DIVA
BLACK WOMEN AUTHORS

Table of Contents

Paulette Henson

Editor Note

FOUNDER
Editor-in-Chief

Dear Readers,

Celebrating the Essence of Black Womanhood: A Journey Through Wo. In the vibrant tapestry of literature, Black women authors have we threads of resilience, wisdom, and beauty, crafting narratives that illumi the rich tapestry of their experiences. BWA Magazine proudly celebrates profound impact of Black women authors, whose voices resonate ac generations, continents, and cultures.

Empowering Narratives: Black women authors stand at the forefror literary excellence, fearlessly exploring themes of identity, heritage, empowerment. Their stories delve deep into the complexities of life, offe insights, inspiration, and hope to readers worldwide. From powerful mem to captivating fiction, each page of BWA Magazine is adorned with brilliance of their storytelling.

Unveiling Untold Stories: Within the pages of BWA Magazine, hid histories are unearthed, and silenced voices are amplified. Black wo authors courageously confront societal injustices, challenge stereotypes, reclaim their narratives with unwavering determination. Their words serv beacons of truth, illuminating the path towards a more inclusive equitable world.

A Platform for Expression: BWA Magazine provides a platform for B women authors to share their stories, celebrate their achievements, connect with a diverse audience of readers. Through thought-provo interviews, insightful essays, and captivating book features, BWA Maga honors the brilliance and resilience of Black women in literature.

Inspiring Future Generations: As torchbearers of literary excellence, B women authors inspire future generations to dream, create, and thrive. T words serve as catalysts for change, sparking conversations, and igni movements for social justice and equality. BWA Magazine is dedicate uplifting and empowering the voices of Black women authors, ensuring their legacies endure for generations to come.

Join the Celebration: Embark on a literary journey like no other with E Magazine. Discover the diverse voices, powerful stories, and transforma wisdom of Black women authors who continue to shape the landscap literature. With each issue, BWA Magazine celebrates the essence of B womanhood and honors the enduring legacy of Black women in literature

BLACK WOMEN AUTHORS
TOP
EMERGING AUTHORS

LEAD BY EXAMPLE
LEADER
GRACIE MCCASTLER

TRANSFORMING INTO AN EFFECTIVE LEADER
GRACIE MCCASTLER
POWER
ENCOUR
LEADER

Educator
Author
Activist

Reconnecting with the Forgotten Fruit
Fruits Of the
SPIRIT
JOY
Peace
Kindness
Self-Control
Faithfulness
Patience
Goodness
Love
A Daily Scriptural Guide to Enha With God
DR. GRACIE KEARSE

Transfor
Truanc
Exploring Factors and Stra
Impact Truancy Among
Dr. Gracie Kearse-M

BWA Author Spotlight
Victoria Anderson

Author

VICTORIA ANDERSON

Victoria Anderson is an emerging voice in the field of self-discovery and empowerment, celebrated for her unique perspective on healing from childhood trauma and defying societal expectations. Her story is deeply intertwined with her own experiences of overcoming obstacles that sought to limit her potential. Growing up in a vibrant yet challenging urban setting, Victoria encountered societal stereotypes that attempted to confine her dreams. However, her unwavering determination to break free from these constraints led her to pursue education as a means of transcending boundaries.

After graduating from a prominent university, Victoria embarked on a personal quest to understand the complexities of childhood trauma and societal pressures. Motivated by her struggles and the stories of individuals she encountered, she devoted herself to extensive research and introspection, seeking ways to facilitate healing and personal growth. Victoria's writing reflects her deep understanding of the human experience, infused with empathy and wisdom. Through her work, she aims to guide others toward self-discovery and overcoming adversity, offering insights and strategies for navigating life's challenges.

BWA Author Spotlight
Victoria Anderson

a passionate advocate for mental health and personal development, Victoria extends

impact beyond her writing. She engages in speaking engagements, captivating

diences with her authentic storytelling and empowering messages. Additionally, she

ively participates in community outreach programs, mentoring and supporting young

ople as they navigate their paths toward resilience and empowerment.

toria Anderson's commitment to fostering healing, reshaping perspectives, and

turing resilience serves as an inspiration to those grappling with childhood trauma and

cietal pressures. Her dedication to igniting transformation and instilling hope continues

nfluence and uplift individuals on their journeys of self-discovery.

Are you an African American looking to create a safe space where you can process your trauma and embrace healing? Would you like to learn how to confront societal pressures effectively, build your resilience, and prioritize yourself? If you've been looking for a book that will empower you to embark on a journey of personal growth and transformation, your search ends here.

More Than Your Trauma is more than just a book about self-discovery for African American women.

It's a comprehensive guide designed to help you accept your ignored experiences, reflect on your struggles, and embrace vulnerability as a path to personal growth and transformation—something that we're often made to feel guilty about.

Not only will your position be acknowledged, but you'll finally learn how to tap into the power of self-care, self-affirmation, and healing to build a life of fulfillment and empowerment.

Through his thought-provoking guide, you'll embrace the importance of prioritizing mental and emotional well-being during adversity, ultimately bringing out the best version of yourself. Are you ready to learn how?

Inside More Than Your Trauma, you'll discover:

"More than your Trauma" is more than just book about self-discovery for African Americ women.

It's a comprehensive guide designed to h you accept your ignoared experiences, refle on your struggles, and embrace vulnerability a path to personal growth and transformation something that we're often made to feel gui about.

Not only will your position be acknowledged, b you'll finally learn how to tap into the power self-care, self-affirmation, and healing to build life of fulfillment and empowerment. Through t thought-provoking guide, you'll embrace t importance of prioritizing mental and emotion well-being during adversity, ultimately bringi out the best version of yourself. Are you ready t learn how?

Doris Pinkett "Pinke Loved"

...sidential Lifetime Achievement Award Recipient, and ...-Published Author of "REFRESHED: A Journey of ...ections and Connections", Doris Pinkett is the founder of ... Pinke Loved Institute, a platform designed to uplift ...men, particularly divorced women as they engage into new ...eriences and reset their lives after divorce. Doris ...ped into the world of writing a few years after her 16-year ...riage shockingly ended due to a $500 disagreement. The ...th and revelations she experienced are penned inside ...book. This Women's Empowerment Speaker has a sincere desire to uplift and ...brate women, as they make a comeback, and excel in every area of their lives. A ...ve of Atlanta, Georgia, and a graduate of the Tennessee State University, Doris is ...proud mother of 3 adult children, Nemiah (24), Melaiah (22) and JaH'son (21), all of ...m are pursuing college degrees, and are leaders in their own right. Whether it be ...ugh her speaking, writing or her "REFRESHED" Yoga series, she aspires to engage, ...ate, encourage, enlighten and empower women so they can maximize their purpose, ...n personally and professionally.

****
20/20 Enterprises Certified
Speaker
Breathe for Change Certified Yoga
and SEL Facilitator
2023 Sisterhood-On-The-Go
Community Service Award
Recipient

**AVAILABLE
ON
AMAZON**

<u>For Bookings and Inquiries</u>:
Phone Number: 404-207-7212
Website: https://linktr.ee/Pinkeloved
Facebook: Pinke Loved
Instagram: pinkelovedinstitute
Email: pinkelovedllc@gmail.com

The Business of Authorship: Navigating the Path to Success by Paulette Henson (*Cont'd*)

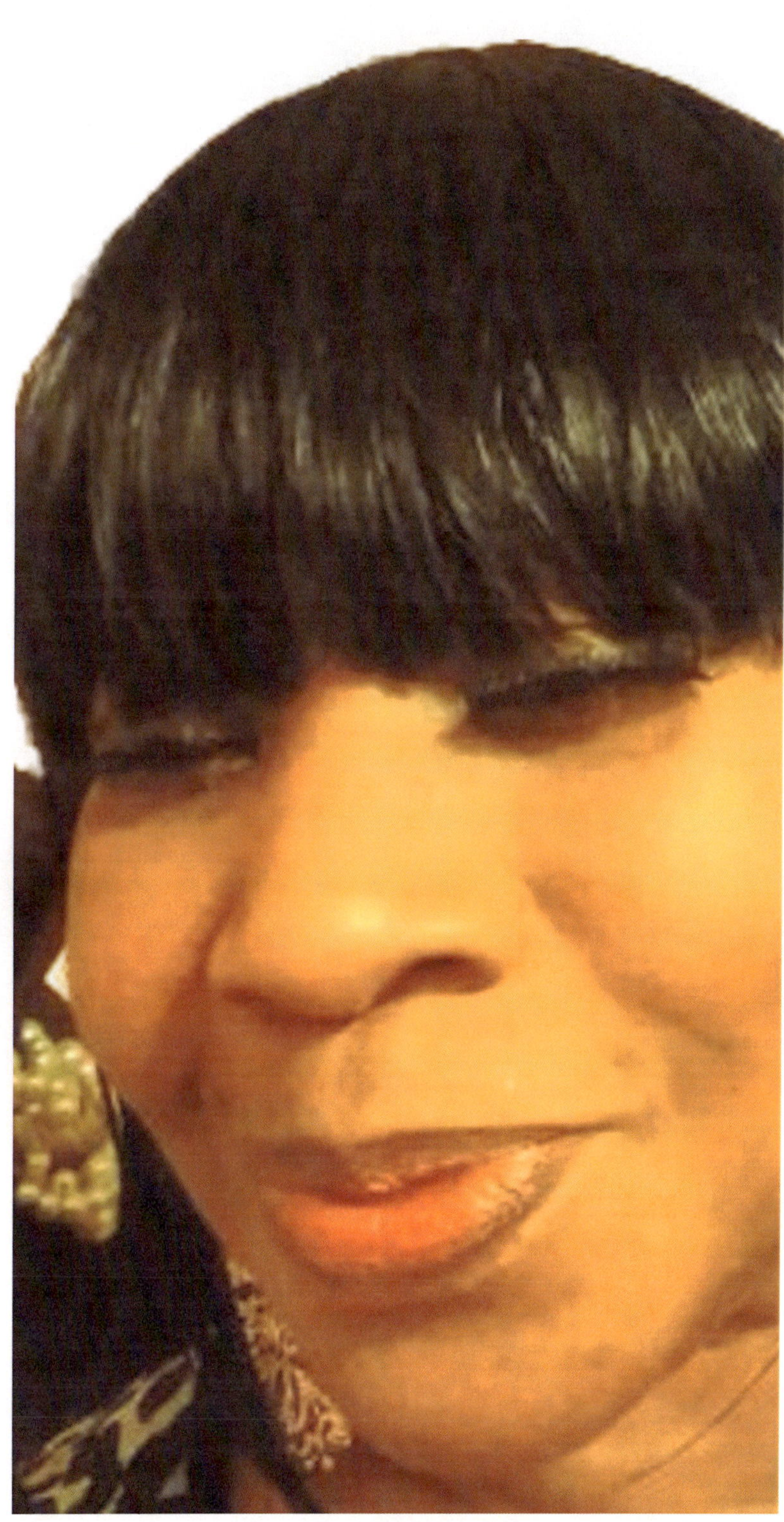

PAULETTE HENSON

Financial Management

Understanding the financial aspects authorship is crucial for long-term succe: Paulette stresses the importance budgeting, keeping track of expenses, a understanding royalties and taxes. "Tre your writing career like a business," s advises. "Keep meticulous records and pl for the future."

Paulette also recommends investing professional services when needed, su as hiring a good editor or a grapl designer for your book cover. "The investments can significantly impact t quality of your work and its reception in t market."

Conclusion

Paulette Henson's journey in the busine of authorship offers invaluable lessons aspiring writers. Her blend of creativi strategic thinking, and entrepreneurial sp has propelled her to success in competitive industry. By viewing authorsh as a business, building a strong persor brand, networking effectively, navigati publishing options, and masteri marketing and financial manageme Paulette has paved the way for others follow.

PAULETTE HENSON"
bwamagazine@gmail.coom

THE BUSINESS OF AUTHORSHIP: NAVIGATING THE PATH TO SUCCESS

Introduction

In the ever-evolving world of publishing, authorship has transcended beyond mere storytelling. It has become a multifaceted business that requires a blend of creativity, strategic planning, and entrepreneurial spirit. Paulette Henson, a successful author and businesswoman, has mastered this art, seamlessly blending her passion for writing with savvy business acumen. In this article, Paulette shares her insights, challenges, and strategies for navigating the business side of authorship.

The Author as an Entrepreneur

When Paulette Henson embarked on her writing journey, she quickly realized that being an author is akin to running a small business. "Writing is just one part of the equation," she explains. "To be successful, you need to think like an entrepreneur." This mindset shift was pivotal in Paulette's career, enabling her to approach her craft with a broader perspective.

Paulette emphasizes the importance of understanding the market and identifying one's target audience. "Knowing who your readers are and what they want is crucial," she says. "It's not just about writing what you love, but also about meeting the needs and interests of your audience." This market-oriented approach has helped Paulette create books that resonate with readers and achieve commercial success.

Building a Brand

One of the cornerstones of Paulette's success has been her ability to build a strong personal brand. "Your brand is your identity as an author," she notes. "It's what sets you apart and makes you recognizable." Paulette's brand is built on authenticity, diversity, and a commitment to quality storytelling.

To establish her brand, Paulette invested time in developing a cohesive online presence. This included a professional website, active social media profiles, and engaging content that reflects her values and style. "Consistency is key," she advises. "Your readers should be able to recognize your voice and message across all platforms."

THE BUSINESS OF AUTHORSHIP: NAVIGATING THE PATH TO SUCCESS

PAULETTE HENSON"
hello@reallygreatsite.com

The Power of Networking

Networking has played a significant role in Paulette's journey. Building relationships with other authors, publishers, and industry professionals has opened doors to new opportunities and collaborations. "Networking is about more than just making connections; it's about creating a supportive community," Paulette explains. "These relationships can provide valuable insights, support, and opportunities for growth."

The importance of attending industry events, joining writer's groups, and participating in online forums. "Being part of a community keeps you informed about industry trends and allows you to share experiences with others who understand your journey."

Navigating Publishing Options

The publishing landscape has evolved dramatically, offering authors multiple pathways to bring their work to market. Paulette has experience with both traditional publishing and self-publishing, and she shares her insights on navigating these options.

"Traditional publishing can prov credibility and wider distribution," says. "However, it often involves a leng process and less control over your wor She would advise authors to caref research publishers and understand terms of any contract before signing.

On the other hand, self-publishing off greater control and potentially hig profits, but it requires a more hands approach. "With self-publishing, you responsible for everything from editing marketing," Paulette explains. "It can challenging, but also incredi rewarding."

Marketing and Promotion

Effective marketing is essential for author. I underscore the importance o comprehensive marketing plan t includes both online and offline strateg "Your book won't sell itself," she asser "You need to actively promote it."

I also utilize social media, em newsletters, book signings, and speak engagements to promote my work. also collaborates with bloggers influencers to reach a wider audience.

"Creative marketing is about find unique ways to connect with your read and keep them engaged," she says.

Author
CHERYL GARRISON

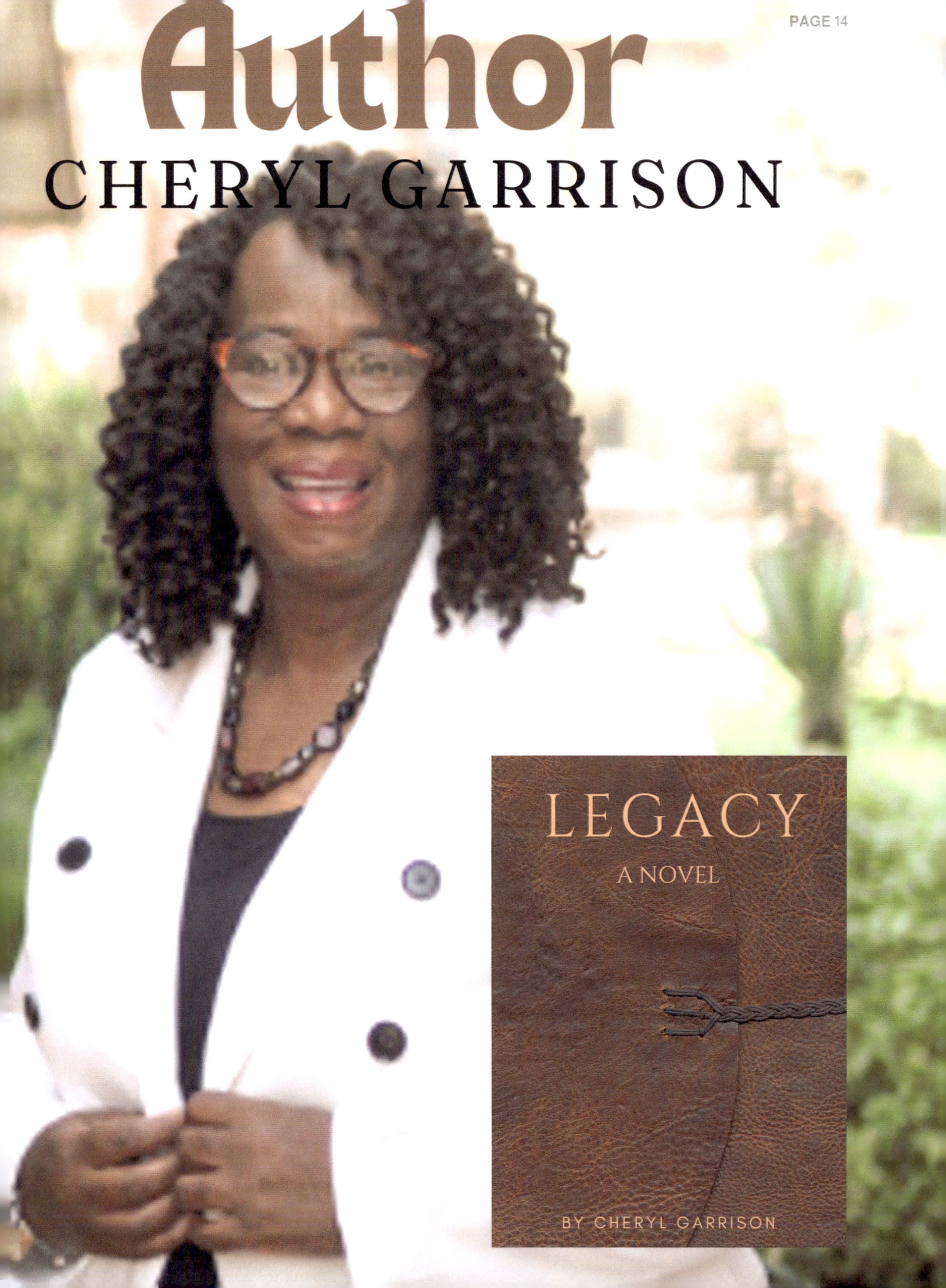

A STORY OF FAMILY, HISTORY, AND THE TRANSFORMATIVE POWER OF TRU

LEGACY
A Novel by Cheryl Garrison

Legacy by Cheryl Garrison is a poignant and compelling novel that delves int intricate dynamics of a modern African American family while uncovering dark and painful legacies of slavery. The story revolves around Marriah, Liz, Nate, Jr., the children of Anna Howard, who has recently passed away. As navigate the emotionally charged task of packing up their childhood hom Phoenix, they stumble upon an old leather-bound journal.

This discovery sets off a series of revelations that deeply impact the siblings. journal, with its timeworn pages, reveals a harrowing secret intertwined with family's history. Among its contents is an old photograph that particu disturbs one of the sisters, forcing her to confront personal demons.

As the siblings delve deeper into the journal, they uncover brutal truths about ancestors' involvement in slavery, including acts of murder. This painful his shakes the very foundation of their identity, bringing to light the often unsp atrocities of the past.

The journey through the journal's revelations is transformative for the sibling compels them to face various personal and familial issues such as sibling riv alcoholism, infidelity, and other hidden secrets that have long simmered ben the surface.

About the Author

Cheryl Garrisonis the CEO of 50Something Lifestyle, a resource, coaching and publishing business for women over 50. She started Becoming 50Something Publications, a publishing wing of her business, to help women over 50 tell their story in a safe and affordable place. She is the author of seven nonfiction books for women over 50 who want to live their BEST life, right now!

Legacy is her first fiction book. For many years, Cheryl has been fascinated with the history of African Americans in this country, from slavery to present-day. She believes that African American families are all shaped by the roots of their ancestors, many of them who were slaves. Most fascinating to Cheryl are the slaves who were able to escape to freedom to a better life of freedom. Legacy is a culmination of Cheryl's passion for history and the legacy of family!

NOW AVAILABLE
https://www.50somethinglifestyle.com/new-releases

Author
KAT NEIL

Kat Neil is a hopeless romantic. She writes contemporary romance and LOVES to read ALL tropes. After many years of devouring happily ever afters, she has finally taken a seat at the writing desk to craft love stories and characters that make her swoon, hoping her readers will swoon along with her. Her debut novel, Love to the Rescue, tells the story of Nicole and Cameron who are on their journey to find love again in a captivating story of healing, trust, and second chances. When Kat is not writing, she is reading, shopping, or watching cooking shows. She is a loving wife and mother to two amazing children. She resides outside of Los Angeles, California.

TRAPPED INTUITION

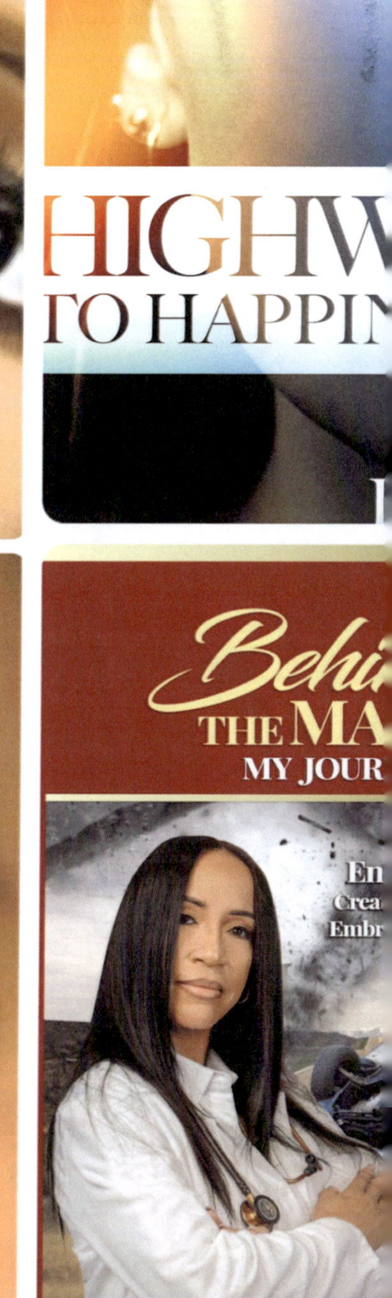
HIGHW
TO HAPPIN
Behi
THE MA
MY JOUR
En
Crea
Embr

Styling
with Josiah
Little Boy
Magic

ADVENTURE
DAYS
with Spain

HOW
START
Clin
Making the impossible b

AUTHOR SPOTLIGHT

About the Author

Ariel a dynamic young woman, has been haunted by a recurring nightmare since childhood where sees the world ending and herself plummeting into hell. Each dream begins differently but inevit ends with the ground collapsing into a fiery abyss that swallows her.

From a young age, Ariel could see spirits that tormented her both awake and asleep, leading to a lifel fear of the dark. Her attempts to share these visions were met with disbelief, forcing her to suffe silence.

In this silence, Ariel struggled with severe alcohol and sex addiction, alongside numerous fa relationships. Her lifelong quest of love, driven by deep-seated issues of paternal abandonment, led to repeated heartbreak. Despite these setbacks, Ariel never lost hope in finding truly love. Howe feeling utterly alone and broken, she often found herself crying out for help even in her sleep, but pleas went unheard. No knight and shining armor came to rescue her.

Confused and desperate, she questioned why she could see spirits when others could not?

In the darkest moments, Ariel contemplated suicide, but ultimately chose to seek life and answers. turned to God, beginning a journey of spiritual warfare to find both love and her true purpose. marked a new chapter in her life, one where she fought for clarity and strength in facing the uns forces that plagued her.

Ariel Cooper
SILENT
SCREAMS

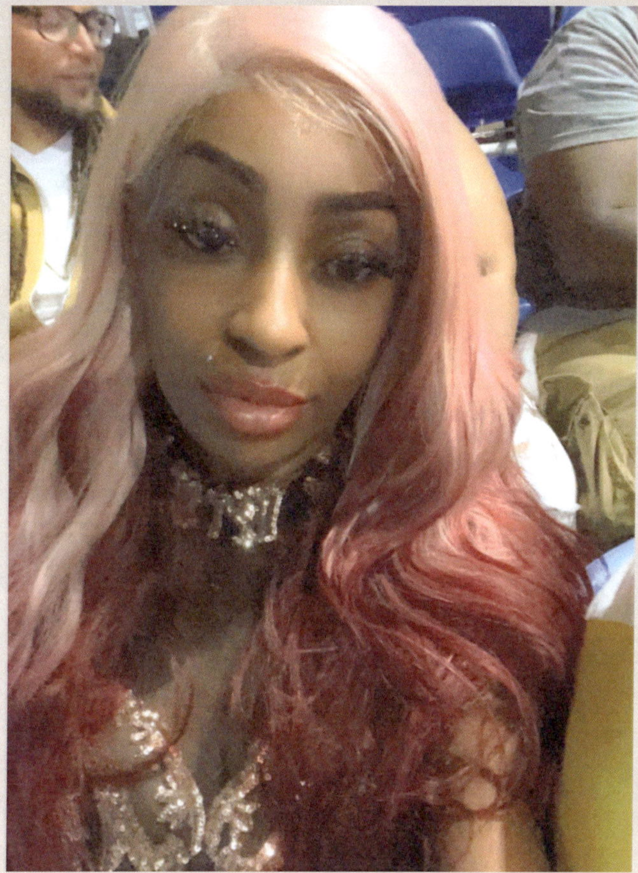

Reception and Future Plans

Since its release, "Silent Scream" has garnered significant atten[tion] and praise. Critics and readers alike commend Cooper's abili[ty to] weave a poignant and gripping narrative that is both relatable [and] enlightening. Her authentic portrayal of trauma and reco[very] resonates deeply, making "Silent Scream" a must-read for an[yone] seeking a story of hope and empowerment.

Ariel Cooper is already hard at work on her next project, which [she] hints will continue to explore themes of resilience and commun[ity.] want to keep telling stories that matter, stories that reflect the struggles and triumphs of our people," she says.

Conclusion

Ariel Cooper's "Silent Scream" is more than just a novel; it is a cla[rion] call for empathy, understanding, and change. By giving a voice to [the] silenced and shining a light on the often-overlooked aspec[ts of] mental health, Cooper not only entertains but also educates [and] inspires. As readers turn the last page, they are left with a rene[wed] sense of hope and a deeper appreciation for the power of storyte[lling.] In a world that often tries to quiet the voices of the marginalized, Cooper's "Silent Scream" reminds us that our stories are pow[erful] and our voices, when found, can change the world.

et's Mission to Empower Women

y, Ariel is on a mission to reach women
g similar challenges. She understands
unique struggles that many women
re, from battling addiction to seeking
ation and love in all the wrong places.
s experiences have equipped her with
mpathy and insight needed to connect
women who feel lost, alone, and
nderstood.

Ariel has begun to speak out more publicly about her journey, sharing her story through writing, speaking engagements, and community outreach. She has started a support group specifically for women who are struggling with addiction, trauma, and spiritual battles. Through this group, Ariel provides a safe space for women to share their experiences, find support, and embark on their own journeys of healing and self-discovery.

In addition to her support group, Ariel is working on a book that delves deeper into her experiences and the lessons she has learned. She hopes that by sharing her story in greater detail, she can reach even more women who need to hear that they are not alone and that there is hope for a better future.

's Journey: From Darkness to Spiritual Awakening

mission is clear: to empower women to reclaim their lives, find their voices, and embrace their true
. She believes that every woman has the potential to overcome her demons and live a life of
se and fulfillment. Through her tireless efforts, Ariel is making a difference, one woman at a time,
g that even the darkest nights can lead to the most radiant dawns.

ory is not just one of personal triumph but a call to action for all women to stand up, speak out, and
rt each other. Ariel's journey is far from over, and as she continues to grow and evolve, she remains

MISS-ADVENTURES LOVE COACHING
EMPOWERING WOMEN ON ALL ASPECTS OF LOVE

Stephanie is a Certified Master Life Coach, the CEO of Miss-Adventures, LLC, three-time #1 Bestselling author, and #1 New Release. Stephanie's mission is empowering women on all aspects of love. She strongly believes in the power of prayer and affirmations to ignite and create the love, health, wealth, success, family, abundance, relationships, and prosperity we want in our lives. Stephanie is a podcaster, public speaker, published writer—over 250 articles between hubpages, Paired Life and Elephant Journal. She has also been a guest on multiple radio and podcast shows. Stephanie has been mentoring women for over 26-plus years and offers in-person and virtual sessions.

STEPHANIE BAILEY

BENEFITS OF SELF-LOVE:

- Personal Growth
- Using your voice—not being afraid to speak up.
- Confronting your fears.
- Empowering yourself through forgiveness—to release being a victim.
- And more…

"Stephanie is an exceptionally valuable expert on relationship advice. Over the years her wisdom and guidance have been at the core of my personal growth on my journey. xoxoxo Love you!"

— NANCY G., COLORADO

CONTACT:

323-332-9976

MISS-ADVENTURES.COM

MISS-ADVENTURES.COM

IS YOUR LOVE WISH LIST KEEPING YOU SINGLE?

STEPHANIE BAILEY

6ft or taller, kind eyes, funny, six-figure incon loves to travel, dark hair, dark complexion, lov opening the door for me, not hairy, loves shoppir intelligent, loves holding my hand, smc vegetarian or pescatarian, drives a BMW Mercedes, a great cook, cleans up after hims strong minded, buys me unique flowers, works o confident, is a planner, looks me in the eyes wh we talk, compassionate, supportive, in great sha straight white teeth, clear complexion, defined al legs, arms and back, mind-blowing sex, w groomed, calls more than texts, not balding, nev argues, loves cats, wants a kid (preferably a gi wants to live near an ocean, generous, gets alo with my friends and family, three to five years old than me, amazing!
A great kisser,Sounds like a lot. Because it is!

Fantasizing about the man you want to marry one day—I get it. Howev making a lengthy list of exactly what he should (and should not) look li sound like, characteristics, traits, career, and financial income is anoth Dating can feel frustrating and hopeless at times, so why are we creating more problematic way for genuine love to come into our lives?

be clear. You should know and understand your five nonnegotiables—the foundations you need for
ccessful relationship. However, if your nonnegotiable includes a man's exact height, race, how
h money he makes, or the car he drives, you will narrowly find lasting love almost impossible.

ast heartbreak making love impossible to find us?

tecting your heart once a man has hurt you is normal and required to make you a wiser dater.
vever, protecting your heart is one thing; locking your heart behind an imaginary vault— made
n some ridiculous list—is another.

ve honestly think that by creating a one-of-a-kind man (on paper) who is the only one (if we
meet him) that can break the code (to this imaginary vault) that's protecting our heart—we will
ng love easier? We won't.

ists subconsciously and intentionally self-sabotage relationships before they even come
our lives. Creating unrealistic expectations that are too long and too specific will only
hen the path to finding love.

lfriend of mine proclaimed she wanted love, but the image she created of what love looks like
e her believe she would never find it. Her list was uniquely very precise.

eeded to be " *ethnic, muscular, an entrepreneur, 6'2 or taller, close to his family, have no*
dren, fashionable, have an income of at least six figures, have a beautiful home, live in an
cale neighborhood, drive a luxury car and is between the ages of forty and fifty years old—
one year younger or older ." Wow. "

n, we can get too caught up in the superficial. Although finances and looks are important, they
t everything. The fact is, looks fade as we get older, and we will lose muscle tone. This doesn't
n that we should be with someone we aren't attracted to. However, if we disbelieve that beauty can
und in someone's personality or expect someone's body to be perfect, then our search becomes
w, which closes the gap to love. The same theory applies to money and finances. Stop.

several difficult breakups and not finding successful love for many years, my friend, decided to
k her list to only include her five nonnegotiable. Once she released the idea of exactly what her
ect" man should look like and opened her heart to meeting a man who treated her well, she ended
eeting her husband.

n, if we find a man perfectly matched to our "paper" idea, he is incompatible with
t our hearts desire and need.

I didn't realize (as many women don't), that I created this list to block myself finding love.

There is no perfect Prince Charming or Ken doll. This type of thinking will er producing a lot of disappointment. Setting the bar too high for what we expec man will only keep us single. Ugh.

Here's the thing: We are not perfect, so why do we hold onto this notion that a should be? Perfect does not exist. Let me repeat myself: Perfect Does Not Exist. If was perfect, we would most likely eventually find him boring. Yet, we will still this image in our heads of exactly what a man should look like and the qualiti should possess—which will inadvertently put a roadblock in our love search.

Ladies, we close ourselves off to love by creating a precise image of our perfec doll. We end up using this "wish list" to hide behind—subconsciously giving u excuse that we are not worthy of ever finding love. We create this list of everythir want and do not want in a man (generally, this list is precise), and then con ourselves, our friends, and family that we really want to find love, be married have children one day—even though our list will make this goal close to impos Hmm... How's that working for you?

Genuine, lasting love will never come in a perfectly wrapped package with a big rec that we created in our heads or on a piece of paper jotted down. If our expectations a specific, we only set ourselves up for major disappointment, heartbreak, and f divorce. Yikes!

What we fail to realize is that men who exhibit superficial and materialistic qualities can tend to be narcissistic, controlling, cheaters, liars, or perhaps will think it's OK to disrespect and emotionally, mentally, or physically abuse us. I've made this mistake before.

Don't get me wrong. I'm not saying all successful men are this way or that being with a financially stable guy isn't essential. God created various types of men in this world for a reason and the beauty we each behold.

Love—with the right match should feel special and unique—not scrutinized and judged.

As women, we proclaim we want love to find us, but often, when love does, we push it away by picking it apart. We ignore obvious *Red Flags* and want men who are completely wrong for us—expecting them to make more effort. We then will reject men who are right for us (if we open our eyes and hearts)—wanting them to try less. We create our bubble of dissatisfaction, then label it, "*I can never find love; there are no good men out there.*" Yikes, what a vicious circle!

Ladies, love is out there. Stop expecting perfection and start appreciating how a man treats you. Love is not meant to be perfect or never have hardships or arguments—that's life. Yes, there needs to be a basic attraction, but not unrealistic. A man's personality will always make him either more or less attractive. When I tore up my list, I found my life partner.

The bottom line is that the rarity is not the wish list you create; it's finding a man who will be there for you emotionally, mentally, physically, spiritually, and financially. Shorten your path to love by being open to letting go of perfection so that the man God intended for you can appear.

GUIDE FOR DEVELOPING YOUR VOICE, CONFIDENCE + PEACE

DAVINA WARD

A QUIET GIRLS' FREEDOM

FEATURED AUTHOR

MICHELE HOSKINS

LEADER
AUTHOR
BUSINESS
WOMAN

PAGE 30

SPEAKERS BIO
MICHELE HOSKINS
SPEAKER | AUTHOR | ENTREPRENUER
PHILANTHROPY EXPERT| KINGDOM WOMAN
WWW.KIRSTENEDUNN.COM

Introducing Michele Hoskins, a seasoned educator, leadership development trainer, and captivating motivational speaker boasting over three decades of enriching experience. Alongside her husband Paul, Michele thrives as an Urban Air Adventure Park Franchisee, expertly managing two bustling parks in San Antonio while eagerly anticipating a thrilling new business venture set to unfold in 2024. Michele's journey epitomizes relentless innovation and purpose-driven action, showcased by her diverse background as a licensed Minister, former McDonald's Franchisee, accomplished Author, College Professor, and dedicated community leader. With the recent launch of Maintain Momentum and the impending release of her forthcoming books, "Unshrunk Bacon" and "Love That Works, Works!", Michele stands as a beacon of excellence in business and leadership. Her expertise extends to designing and implementing successful business models, fueled by her strategic vision and profound understanding of organizational dynamics. Beyond her professional endeavors, Michele's passion for growth and empowerment shines through in her commitment to community upliftment, actively supporting non-profits, educational initiatives, and church endeavors. Currently nearing completion of her second doctorate in Educational Leadership - Organizational Management from Brenau University, Michele's thirst for knowledge and academic achievement further enhances her impressive repertoire, complemented by a Master's Degree in Educational Leadership and a Bachelor of Arts in Business Administration. Outside of her professional pursuits, Michele finds joy in dancing, reading, and embarking on adventures with her husband Paul, twins Hayley

Welcome to the world of *Unshrunk Bacon*.

Michele Hoskins invites you on a journey of empowerment and resilience. Through her own experiences and insights, she offers valuable lessons on navigating life's challenges without shrinking or withdrawing.

Michele's passion for equipping others to overcome obstacles shines through as she shares practical strategies and heartfelt encouragement. Whether you are facing personal setbacks, professional hurdles, or unexpected twists in your journey, *Unshrunk Bacon* provides a roadmap for embrading resilience, fostering growth, and savoring the fullness of life.

Join Michele as she guides you toward a life of strength, courage, unyielding determination, and faith.

MICHELE HOSKINS

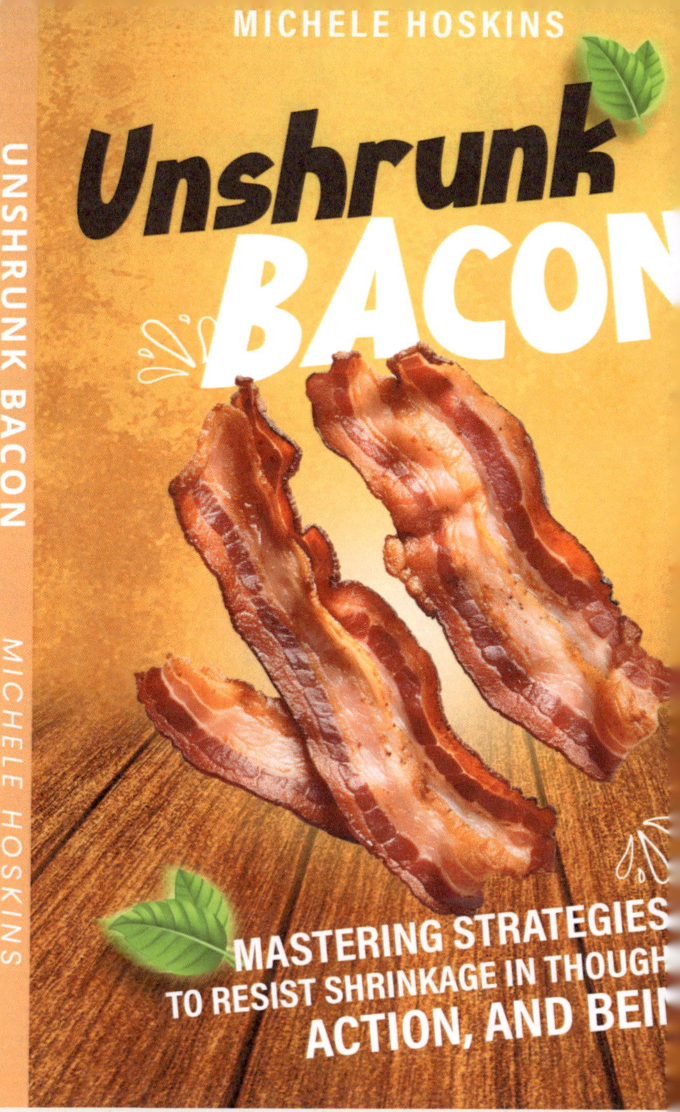

Available on Amazon.com

Manifesting Your Best Life
90 DAY MANIFESTING JOURNAL
JENNIFER BROWN

DENISE W. THARPE

Authentic Self-Published Author

Denise W. Tharpe is a five time author and storyteller. She was born in Gary Indiana. She has been an educator for over 20 years, which is what encouraged her to become an Author. Denise has a Bachelors of Art degree in Business Administration from Strayer University. She has been married to her husband Vincent for over 38 years, and together they have three beautiful adult children. Denise's desire is to continue her journey in writing Children books that will be an encouragement to all people, especially children. It is her hope to be the best that she can be and encourages others to do the same.

Educator and Children's Book Author

Email: dsstylemarketplace@yahoo.com

website: denisetharpe.my.canva.site

Facebook - Authentic Author Denise Tharpe

901-290-8387

BWA
AUTHOR
SPOTLIGHT

AUTHOR CHERIKA SHIELDS

Cherika Shield is a Certified Life Coach and a dedicated Nurse by profession. Above all, she is a child of God, whose faith and experiences have shaped her life's journey. Inspired by the transformative power of God's grace, Cherika has penned her first book. Through her writing, she aims to share her story of empowerment and transformation through faith, hoping to inspire and uplift others on their own journeys spiritually and mentally.

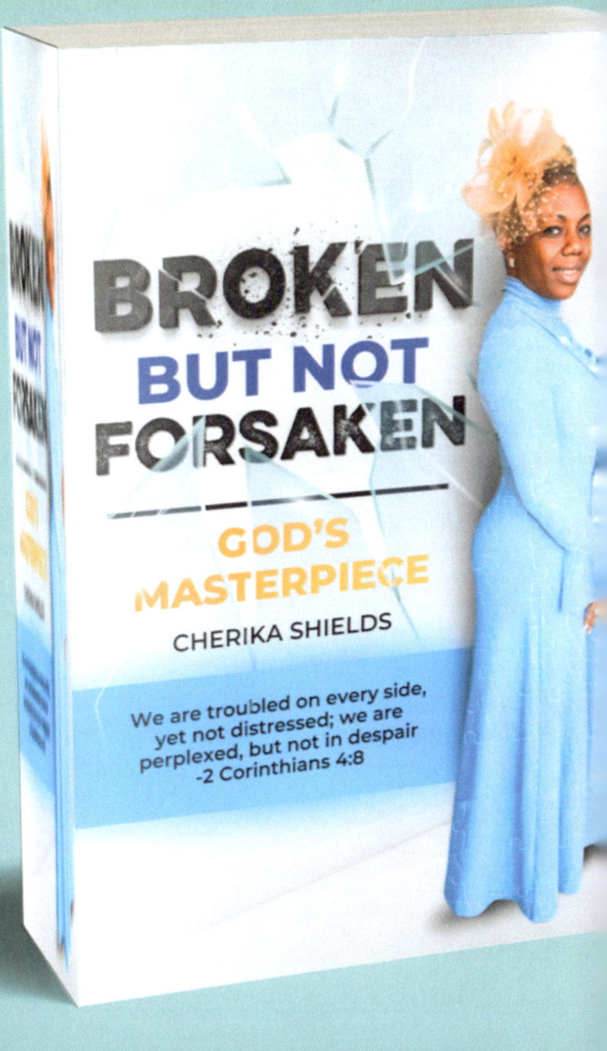

The Author's Lounge Interview with
Cherika Shields

Cherika Shields: Author, Nurse, and Beacon of Hope
Introducing Cherika Shields and Her Inspiring Book

rika Shields is not just an author; she beacon of hope and resilience. Her , "Broken But Not Forsaken," is a ment to the human spirit's ability to come adversity and find strength in face of life's most challenging mstances. As a dedicated nurse, ika has spent years caring for the ical well-being of her patients. ever, she recognized that true ng often requires more than just ical care. This realization led her to "Broken But Not Forsaken," a book offers both physical and mental e.

Journey of "Broken But Not aken"

ken But Not Forsaken" is more than title; it encapsulates the essence of ika's mission to provide hope and ouragement to those who feel lost broken. The book is a collection of nal anecdotes, reflections, and tical advice that guides readers gh the process of healing and self-very. Cherika's compassionate and athetic approach resonates deeply readers, making her book a source mfort and strength.

A Conversation on The Author's Lounge Podcast

Cherika Shields recently joined us on The Author's Lounge Podcast, where she shared her journey as a writer and her passion for nursing. During the interview, Cherika spoke candidly about her motivations for writing "Broken But Not Forsaken." She emphasized the importance of addressing both physical and mental health, drawing from her experiences as a nurse to illustrate how interconnected these aspects of well-being are.

Cherika recounted stories from her nursing career, highlighting moments when she provided not only medical care but also emotional support to her patients. These experiences reinforced her belief that words of encouragement and a listening ear can be just as healing as any medication. Her dedication to holistic care is evident in both her professional life and her writing.

Conclusion: Embracing Hope and Healing
Cherika Shields is a shining example of how one person can make a profound difference in the lives of others. Through her book, "Broken But Not Forsaken," and her work as a nurse, she continues to inspire and uplift those around her. Her interview on The Author's Lounge Podcast was a heartfelt exploration of her journey and mission, leaving listeners with a sense of hope and encouragement.

CALM, FOCUS, AND INSPIRATION

by Victoria Pearson

As I sit down to write this article, I take a moment to center myself, reflecting on my journey into mindfulness. It's a path I stumbled upon not through any grand epiphany but through a much more personal connection – my daughter.

I watched in awe as my daughter transformed and elevated her life through the practice of mindfulness for the past ten years. Her increased focus, reduced stress, personal and professional accomplishments, and overall sense of well-being were impossible to ignore. Seeing these changes in her sparked my curiosity. Could mindfulness offer similar benefits to my life?

While I'm still at the beginning of my mindfulness journey, I've already discovered valuable insights that I'm eager to share with you about mindfulness and its potential to enhance the craft of writing and your life, overall.

Understanding Mindfulness for Writers

At its core, mindfulness is about being fully present in the moment, aware of our thoughts and surroundings without judgment. For writers, this state of heightened awareness can be a gateway to deeper creativity, improved focus, and a wellspring of inspiration.

As I've begun to practice mindfulness, I've noticed how it helps quiet the constant chatter in my mind – you know, that inner critic that never seems to take a day off. It's creating space for new ideas to emerge and allowing me to approach demanding activities, such as building my business, grokly me, with renewed

The Science Behind Mindfulness

While my initial interest came observing my daughter, I've since l that there's solid science backing benefits of mindfulness. Studies shown that regular mindfulness p can actually change our brains, incr gray matter in areas linked to le memory, and emotional regulation.

For writers, this translates to im cognitive flexibility, better concent and an enhanced capacity for emp all crucial elements in crafting com narratives and connecting with readers.

Practical Applications in Writing

As I've started integrating mindfulne my routine, I've discovered a few pr that seem particularly helpful in you today lives, especially when writing:

- Mindful Writing Sessions: Befo start writing, take a few minu focus on your breath. It's amazir this simple act can clear my mir prepare you for focused v Sensory Awareness: When des scenes or characters, try tc engage your senses. What wou smell, hear, or feel if you were This deepened awareness wil

Victoria Pearson

This deepened awareness will bring more vivid details to your writing.

Focused Free Writing: Set a timer for 10-15 minutes and write without stopping, focusing solely on the act of writing. It will help you bypass your inner critic and tap into a more creative flow.

Mindful Observation: Learn to observe your surroundings more attentively. Whether you're in a busy café or a quiet park, try to notice details you might have missed before. It will provide rich material for your writing.

Overcoming Challenges

I'll be honest – incorporating mindfulness into my routine hasn't been without its challenges. Most days, my mind feels particularly restless, or when finding time for practice seems impossible amidst numerous deadlines and other responsibilities.

On those days, I remind myself of the changes I saw in my daughter, and I start small. Sometimes it's just three conscious breaths before I write, or a mindful walk around the block to clear my head. I'm learning that consistency matters more than perfection.

Looking Ahead

I am particularly interested in learning how others incorporate mindfulness into their and their lives, overall. Does your mindfulness practice enhance your writing or the process? Or does it help in managing the emotional ups and downs of a writing car balancing hectic personal and professional responsibilities? Share your thoughts, tip experiences with others on the BWA Facebook page.

Conclusion

While I'm still new to the world of mindfulness, I'm already seeing its potential to tran my approach to life as a whole. Just as it did for my daughter, mindfulness is opening u perspectives and possibilities for me.

I invite you, my fellow writers, to join me on this journey. Whether you're a sea mindfulness practitioner or a curious newcomer like me, there's room for all of us to gro learn together.

Let's explore how mindfulness can enrich our lives and our writing, one breath, one w a time. I'd love to hear about your experiences or answer any questions you might have all, we're in this together – not just as writers, but as humans striving to bring more awar and authenticity to our craft and our lives.

If you are inclined to learn more about mindfulness or the step-by-step process yo follow to becoming a self-published author, take advantage of your BWA affiliation and in the grokly.me Writer's Workshop while the classes are FREE. Send an email to Paule to me (admin@grokly.me) and we'll get you enrolled.

Here's to our continuing journey of discovery through mindfulness and writing.

SHENITA L YELL

CO-AUTHOR

THE TARNISHED CROWN

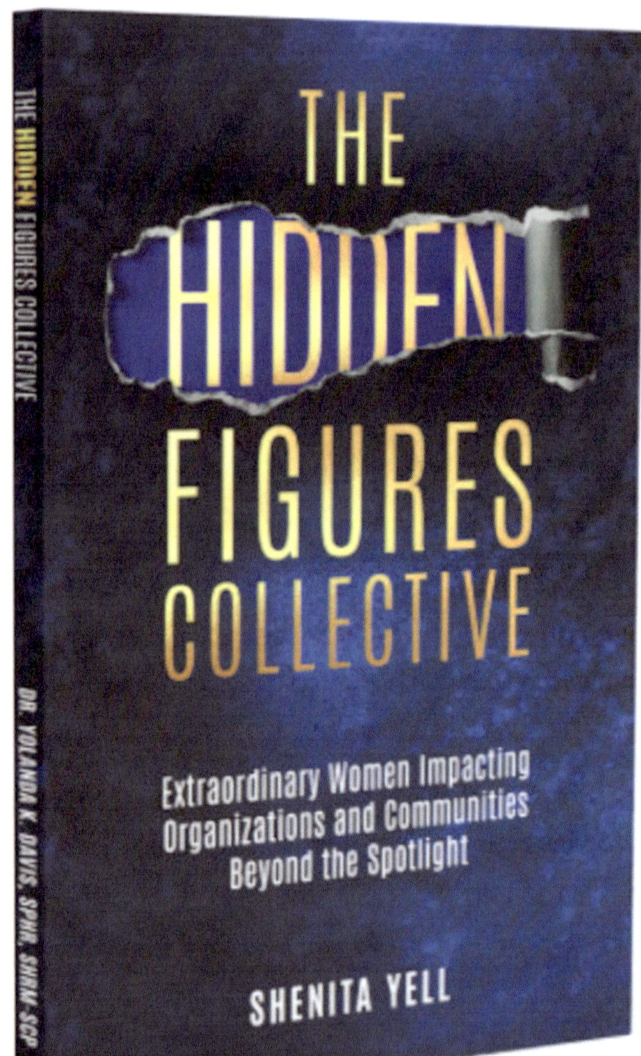

AUTHOR

CHANTELLE CROWELL

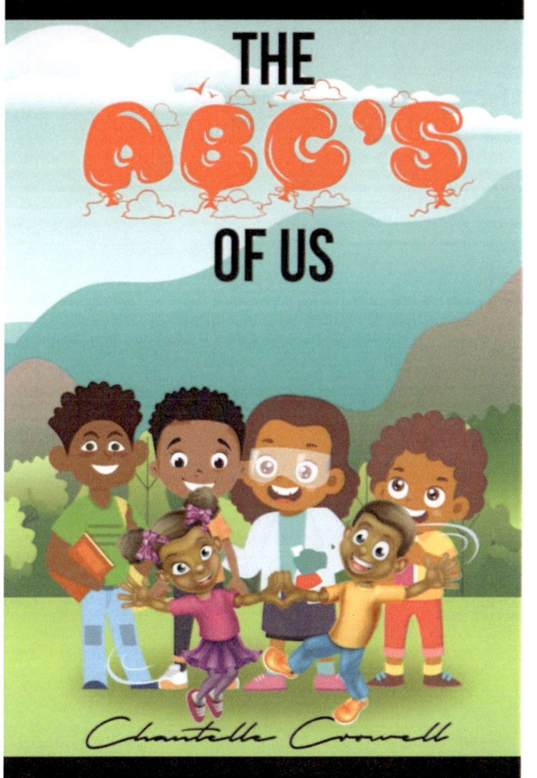

Graduating from Central Piedmont Commun[ity] College was a defining moment in my life, [a] testament to my unwavering commitment a[nd] perseverance. Balancing the rigorous deman[ds] of studying to become a Nurse Assistant, Nota[ry] Republic, and Medication Technician wh[ile] simultaneously caring for my six childr[en] required immense dedication. Yet, with t[he] unwavering support of my beloved family by [my] side, I was fortified with the strength [to] overcome every obstacle. Their love a[nd] encouragement became the cornerstone of [my] success, fueling my determination to achieve [my] dreams. Writing became more than just [a] hobby; it became my lifeline, a sanctuary whe[re] I could retreat and let my thoughts flow free[ly] onto the page. Inspired by the bedtime storie[s] shared with my children, I discovered a passi[on] for children's literature. As an African-Americ[an] woman, I recognized the importance [of] representation in the stories that children rea[d.] I wanted to create characters and narrativ[es] that reflected the diverse experiences and ri[ch] cultural heritage of my community. Each wor[d] penned was a reflection of my innerm[ost] thoughts and experiences, woven together li[ke] threads in a tapestry. Through the art [of] storytelling, I found solace and meanir[g,] transforming the ordinary moments of my li[fe] into extraordinary narratives. Each stroke of t[he] pen was a testament to my resilience and t[he] depth of my spirit, a celebration of the journ[ey] that had brought me to this moment.

AUTHOR
Davina Ward

Davina Ward is an Author and Certified Christian Life Coach commissioned by God to free women and help them understand that resilience is possible - no matter what they have endured. She has experienced a vast array of challenges that have authenticated and motivated her to share her experiences with other vulnerable women.

She commonly refers to herself as the P.U.S.H. Coach, (Persist, Until, Satan, Halts), due to her effective coaching approach that guides women into learning how to discover and tap into their purpose through the tearing down of their limiting beliefs and insecurities.

Her program and teachings provide strategies to remove layers of lies, doubt, and shame that paralyze women of purpose.

Davina partners with her clients as they shift their focus from the reflection they see in the mirror to the warrior God designed them to be in the spirit. Her main goal is personal development leaving her clients feeling equipped and worthy to walk into what God has purposed them to do and be.

Her true passion lies in walking beside vulnerable women to awaken their inner selves as they enter into their destiny.

In addition to her life's work, Davina has an extensive background in the public sector working with individuals with modest means. She was born and raised in New Jersey and resides with her husband, Reverend Robert Ward. She delights in being a mother to 3 sons and a grandmother to 2 grandchildren. She delights in serving in her local church and community.

Author
Erica N. Bryant

Erica N. Bryant is a wife and mother of two. She is an elementary educator and literacy advocate. Erica is the president and founder of Sparrow's Song Ministries (Sparrowssongministries.com), a group of believers who "just love Jesus." Her campaign: "The Word W.O.R.K.S." have helped women renew and strengthen their relationship with God by falling in love with His Word. Erica serves faithfully at her home church, Strait Gate Deliverance Center, where her father, Bishop Jerome Rogers, is pastor.

Author

Dr. Lisa L. Campbell

Dr. Lisa L. Campbell, known as "The Growth Motivator™," is the author of the inspirational book "Grow With Me." In this book, Dr. Lisa shares her journey of overcoming significant personal and professional challenges. Through vivid storytelling and heartfelt reflections, she shares her life lessons on resilience, faith, and personal growth. Her journey as an author began with a desire to inspire others, and she has developed a motivational writing style that connects deeply with readers. "Grow With Me" encourages readers to shed the weight of their burdens, embrace change, and pursue their dreams with determination and confidence. Dr. Lisa's engaging narrative and genuine voice make her book an uplifting and transformative read.

Author
Lena Lee

LENA M. LEE, a native of southeastern Pennsylvania developed her love for writing, art, fashion and inventions at an early age. In 2000, Lee was awarded a utility patent for dolls she created that were of no race or nationality for both boys and girls called "The Lollipop Tots" and has written 16 short stories about the dolls. Her first published of the series, The Lollipop Tots -The Great Parade. She is also the published author of "Panic in the Jungle" and has a patent pending for a multifunctional laptop invention which she won first place at West Chester University in 2014 for most innovative new idea. In her spare time, Lee enjoys reading, drawing and spending time with her family.

Overcoming *Writers* Block

Valerie Staton

term "Writer's Block" was popularized by psychoanalyst Edmund Bergler, who used it in his "The Writer and Psychoanalysis" published in 1947. Since then, "writer's block" has become a ly recognized term in the creative community, describing the frustrating and often debilitating nomenon that writers may encounter. So, now that we know a little historical fact about the term r's block, what are some things we can do when confronted with it?

gage in Physical Activity: Taking a break from writing and engaging in physical activity can help rs relieve stress. Whether it's going for a walk, doing yoga, or hitting the gym, exercise can boost orphins and reduce anxiety, allowing writers to return to their work with a refreshed mindset.

actice Mindfulness or Meditation: Spending a few minutes practicing mindfulness or meditation niques can help writers relax and clear their minds. This can be as simple as focusing on deep thing or using guided meditation apps to promote relaxation and reduce stress.

ead for Pleasure: Reading books, articles, or blogs unrelated to the writer's current project can de a much-needed escape. By immersing themselves in another author's words, writers can nspiration, gain new perspectives, and give their minds a break from their own writing.

plore Other Creative Outlets: Engaging in other creative activities like painting, cooking, drawing, ng a musical instrument. These activities can stimulate different parts of the brain and help writers to their creativity from a different angle.

onnect with Fellow Writers: Joining writing groups, attending workshops, or participating in e forums can create a sense of community and support. Interacting with other writers who erstand the challenges of writer's block can provide encouragement, advice, and a fresh ective.

Overcoming *Writer's* Block! *Cont'd*

by Valerie Staton

6. Take a Break and Rest: Sometimes, the best way to relieve stress during writer's bloc take a complete break from writing. This could involve going on a short vacation, spe time with loved ones, or simply resting and rejuvenating.

7. Practice Self-Care: Taking care of oneself is crucial during periods of writer's block. Th involve getting enough sleep, eating well, staying hydrated, and engaging in activitie bring joy and relaxation. Prioritizing self-care can help writers maintain a healthy mindse overcome the stress associated with writer's block.

Remember, writer's block is a common challenge that many writers face, and finding w relieve stress and foster creativity is unique to each individual. Experiment with dif techniques and discover what works best for you to overcome writer's block and inspiration once again.

Native New Yorker Living in Rhode Island Celebrates the Success of Her First Book

Photography by Craig A. Kirkland
Great Amazement Multimedia Entertainment LLC

CLARISE ANNETTE BROOKS knew from a young age that she could spark magic when she put pen to paper. "I recall when our teachers would give us creative writing assignments in elementary school. We each had to take turns reading our work at the front of the room. My classmates often requested that I go first," Clarise recalls. "I knew I had them when they laughed at the right moment, gasped at the right time, and talked with me later about the characters I had created or about the poetry that I had just performed for them. It came easy to me and I enjoyed it SO MUCH. It has always been fun to use imagery to create a scene, alliteration to develop a flow of words, or repetition to demand emphasis. These tools of the language helped me to take my classmates on a journey with me and planted the seed for my lifelong love of performing my work before a live audience. I learned how to use language and its tools to touch the minds and spirits of others."

Poetry is Life!

Poetry, often described as the language of the soul, has a unique ability to transcend time, culture, [and] circumstance, leaving an indelible mark on the hearts and minds of those who encounter its ve[rses]. Beyond the rhythmic words and metaphors lies a profound power that has shaped societies, mo[ved] nations, and connected individuals on a deeply emotional level. Let's delve into the mystical wor[ld of] poetry and explore the extraordinary power it holds.

1. The Healing Elixir: Poetry possesses a remarkable therapeutic quality. In times of sorrow, it can be a soo[thing] balm, offering solace and a means of expression for emotions too profound for ordinary words. The act of cr[eating] verses can be cathartic, helping individuals process grief, anxiety, or even joy, and find inner peace throug[h self] expression.

2. The Bridge Between Souls: Poetry has a unique ability to connect people across cul[tural,] linguistic, and geographical divides. It transcends the boundaries of language, allowing individuals [of] diverse backgrounds to understand and empathize with one another's experiences. It serves [as a] universal language that reminds us of our shared humanity.

3. A Lens to the World: Poets often act as society's mirrors, reflecting its beauty, flaws, [and] contradictions. Through verse, they shed light on societal issues, injustices, and human condition[s that] might otherwise remain unseen. Poetry challenges the status quo and fosters a collective awaren[ess,] driving change and sparking movements for justice and equality.

4. The Dance of Imagination: Poetry is a playground for imagination. It encourages us to see [the] world through fresh eyes, to explore the mysteries of existence, and to question the norms of socie[ty. It] unlocks the doors to creativity, inviting us to wander through the realms of fantasy and the possib[ilities] of the unknown.

5. A Timeless Legacy: Poems are timeless treasures. The verses of poets from centuries [ago] continue to resonate with readers today. The enduring quality of poetry lies in its ability to capture [the] essence of the human experience, making it relevant across generations and eras.

A Vehicle for Social Change: Poetry has historically played a pivotal role in ving social change. Poets like Langston Hughes, Maya Angelou, and Pablo Neruda ed their verses to advocate for civil rights, equality, and justice. Through their rds, they ignited movements and inspired generations to stand up for what they lieved in.

. The Elevation of Language: Poetry elevates language to an art form. It nonstrates the beauty of precision and the magic of metaphor. Poets carefully ect words, creating a symphony of sounds and meanings that delight the senses d challenge the mind.

. An Echo of Identity: Poetry is a profound expression of identity. It allows ividuals to embrace and celebrate their cultural heritage, personal experiences, d individual uniqueness. It serves as a repository of cultural memory, preserving ditions and stories for future generations.

a world often dominated by prose and pragmatism, poetry stands as a testament the enduring power of human creativity and expression. It serves as a bridge ween hearts, a beacon of hope, and a catalyst for change. Through its profound lity to heal, connect, and inspire, poetry remains a force that continues to shape world, one verse at a time.

Authentically You!

A New Thing!

Hello readers. It's Stella Stella. I hope you read the short introduction piece in t
BWA/BMA Newsletter. Just in case, here it is again, this time with more details.
Our objective - What do BWA readers think about a column for us, by us, abo
us?

After brainstorming different ideas and concepts, we thought of starting rig
here, with a simple and straight forward introduction, and let's see where we g
The idea being we'll come up with our own authentic and organic foru
collectively.

Allow me to introduce myself and tell you a bit about me since I'll be on t
receiving end of your feedback.

I am a regular person, I am not wealthy and certainly not famous. However, I
have a few experiences to share, in hopes of engaging and inspiring you, in son
way.

For example, like many of you, I love writing. I am not among famous Literarie
but that's okay.

My whereabouts – the abbreviated short version is that I'm currently in Texas
by way of California.

he longer version is I am originally from California (shout out to Bay Area Folks). worked thirty-two years doing a nine-to-five job in the healthcare industry. I ways believed there was more to life than work-work-work, commuting, a little t of home life and sleep, then more work - 😌 Anyway you get the picture.

A few years ago, I retired from my job/work. I was ready to leave the entire rat ce, the commute, the daily grind, the never having time for myself, and so on. bout a year prior to retiring, in preparation for our next chapter, my husband nd I became groupies of HGTV and Travel channels. We were assessing ossibilities for our future lives in retirement. Our kids were adults and living eir own lives. So, it was kind of natural that we began to contemplate moving – nly in our case we were considering moving to another country. ondering the idea of living abroad also made me realize that I still had a lot of e ahead of me. I had a new luxury brewing, and that luxury was time. s we became more engrossed with the idea of living in a different country, both us set our priority for a warm climate and a simple life. Another must have for e was having access to some version of a shopping mall. e did some research, visited a few places, and then we jumped.
✦

First, we spent a month on the Camino De Santiago, which is a spiritual lgrimage that starts in France, and culminates in Spain. After that endeavor, ur jump took us to the Caribbean, where we checked out a few places and ded up staying a few months, then finally (almost) we decided to settle ermanently in Mexico.

We had been living in Mexico, happy and content, for a year and a half, until e global pandemic happened. Suddenly we were overwhelmed with certainty about everything; as expats we had established residency, but we ere still foreigners. We had not yet learned all the bureaucracies or the ealthcare systems, we were still new to the culture and learning traditions, and e were not fluent in Spanish.

As the shutdowns were fast approaching, we became laser focused to return the United States, as urgently as possible. The news was reporting that eople in our age group or higher were at significant risk. Our plans of remaining road were abandoned. We ruled out returning to California because it was too xpensive. And so, we chose Texas.

abundance of time, I now pick and choose what I want to do, or not. One of my
in-the-sky' passions is to write, and so, I do. Little 'ole me - I even had the aud
to pitch a collab with BWA Magazine. If they had said no, I was prepared t
again, and again. But, they said let's chat, and here we are.
So, that's a bit about me. How are y'all?

   I know, I know, that was an exact repeat of the Newsletter short. It was purp
posted the same because it included the introduction - in case anyone miss
Now, let's dive into some detailed information.
First, about the Camino De Santiago spiritual pilgrimage –

   Toward the end of our work careers, naturally we began to ponder our
chapter of retirement. We had our own individual goals and hobbies, as well a
combined goals and hobbies. We were pondering our new thing; a diff
lifestyle, learning a different country, new pace, new income status (pe
income is lower than salaried income) etc.

   It was a lot to think about and at times it was daunting. But we felt we
ready. ✦

   The idea of walking the Camino De Santiago initially presented itself to us ju
chance. We learned of the Camino through my son's high school assignmer
husband and I were equally intrigued with the principle and purpose o
pilgrimage. Most people do it for religious and/or spiritual reasons.

   In our case, we embraced the spiritual aspect of the pilgrimage and thou
would be a good opportunity to take the time and settle our souls before sta
our next chapter. A sort of "let's consider every aspect…".

   We also learned that there are several different Camino routes to choose fr
Once we decided on doing the Camino pilgrimage, our first mission wa
research and train. Neither of us had ever done something like this before an
were not sure what to expect. My husband did most of our research.

   Our initial inclination was to learn and research everything down to every c
the terrain, weather, altitudes, sleeping, eating, what about emergencies, int
access, a different currency, a different culture, and so on. But, as we gained
understanding about the intention and significance of the Camino, our cau
attitudes relaxed.

We decided on the most popular French route which starts in Saint
Port, France, and ends at the famous Cathedral in Santiago, Spain. It
only needed to make decisions on three concerns. (1) Choosing wh...
Choosing our backpacks, hiking shoes and miscellaneous gear. And last, (3) we
ew we needed to train for the physical aspect, at least some walking and hiking.
t was it! By design, the Camino pilgrimage will provide whatever else you
ght need.

We developed our mindsets to not be fixed on expectations. Especially, the
ly flow and routines in the way we already knew; we get up, get ready for work,
nmute to and from, maybe some errands or other business, figure out meals,
. However, for the Camino, none of that flow or routine would be a factor
ause for the entire journey, we would be living out of our respective
kpacks, and we would be walking.

With our new adjusted and relaxed mindsets, we felt more prepared. We had
visions to keep warm and dry, we would find modest sleeping arrangements
food along the way. Whatever else, we would be open to the experience.

he Camino De Santiago "French Route" - It is approximately 800 kilometers, or
miles long. On average it takes between 35-45 days to complete, depending
your daily walking distance and rest days. In our case, we had a total of about
ty-five days for our entire journey. We also decided that following our Camino
rimage, we would remain in Spain and spend a few days in Barcelona before
rning home in the U.S. Essentially, in order to fit all of this into thirty-five days,
had to reduce the number of days actually on the Camino.

We set off for France, just the two us. We ended up spending twenty-six days
the Camino pilgrimage, and it was a wonderful and epic experience. So much
that we are doing it again in 2025.

Along the Camino, we met people from all over the world. Neither my husb
or I spoke French, Spanish, nor any other foreign language, yet communica
was never an issue. It was a beautiful journey of time and simplicity, and it
priceless. Just one of the beauties of this pilgrimage is that each per
experiences it differently. My husband's experience was not the same as m
yet we equally loved it.

By the end of our Camino, a huge epiphany for us was our certainty to m
into our next chapter of life, which included moving to another country.

Each day on our Camino, I journaled our experience and shared it with
friends back at home in the U.S. They insisted I publish it, so I did. It is availabl
Amazon - A Personal Journey: 26 Days Traveling The Camino De Santiago, by St
Stella.

My husband and I are planning another Camino in 2025. If this is something
are interested in doing, I recommend first watching the 2010 movie titled '
Way' with Martin Sheen and Emilio Estevez. This movie is a very realistic
accurate depiction of the Camino.

Also, a great book of information is by John Brierley, titled 'A Pilgrim's Guide to
Camino De Santiago'.

After our work careers, we planned a quick visit to the North Coast of the

minican Republic. It was a destination we considered for retirement. Our

ention was to stay ten days. It was such an enjoyable and peaceful time for

Long story short, we ended up staying a few months.

It is important in life to continue making new memories. I learned this in

 D.R. We were there over a Thanksgiving Holiday, and it became one of my

orite Thanksgiving memories.

 now, I will be brief on our stay in the D.R. and save the details for the

vember issue of BWA.

✦

ow is a snapshot of where we stayed in Cabarete, D.R.

Retiring in Mexico / South of the Border –

The overall experience was nice. I don't mention my husband in many of
stories because that is his preference. While I am outgoing, he is more of
introvert who enjoys being at home. However, he was/is always there, 'so
distancing' -

When I/We first arrived in Cabo San Lucas, my feeling was neutral. I was exc
and looking forward to the experience of living in a different country. I did not k
anyone, I did not speak any Spanish, and I knew nothing about Mexico. I had
expectations other than I was looking forward to a positive experience and an e
lifestyle.

In our case, the retirement home we purchased was not ready, so we lived
residential apartment portion of a hotel, which is a common practice in Mexic
was basic with modest accommodations, and it had a wonderful view of
gorgeous blue ocean and beaches. From our balcony we could see cruise s
coming in and out of the harbor, but more spectacular, especially during wh
season, you could see them swim by, noticeably spouting out water. Sometime
would be a single whale, and other times there was a group of them. It was alwa
captivating sight.

Being immersed in the culture we quickly learned the local Mexican people
an appreciation for nature. Basic elements like sunshine, the ocean, and natu
grown foods (produce/cactus/tequila) were a source of pride. Inexpensive ta
and seafood were always delicious, and always prepared fresh, not processed.
I am fairly outgoing, so it did not take long for me to make friends. I met a
amigas that I saw regularly, and we developed a mutual friendship. I became t
hermana (sister). I am also a licensed esthetician, and eventually, I worked tw
three days each week in a beauty spa with them. They did beauty and spa serv
for locals and tourists, while I did microblading.

My amigas' English was equally lacking with my Spanish, yet we all managed.
had plenty of laughs when either of us were off by a word or two. It was alwa
good time.

plenty of laughs when either of us were off by a word or two. It was always a good

e.

Technically I was an expatriate, or expat, and could go about as expats did.
vever, my amigas showed me how locals lived. They showed me more secluded
ches, where they shopped, went to see movies, and so on. Most days we would go
for lunch, even if only to a very delicious food stand. And, at night or on
kends, they took me to their favorite spots, sometimes in a residential area where
eone's backyard was transitioned into a popup restaurant, complete with take-
service. (Just a quick memory – my favorite tamales were from a guy who sold
n right out of pots, at his stand, which was located on a sidewalk in front of a tire
o. On weekends or holidays there would be a long line for his tamales).
eing immersed in the culture I had many wonderful experiences and memories. I
ned to keep a beach blanket in the back of my car for routine and spontaneous
ch stops. And, because I am such a "Foodie", I learned to make authentic tamales,
my amigas, at their house. I celebrated Rosca de Reyes, which I previously knew
ing about. I learned about Chiles en Nogada, which is a classic Latin dish made
red, white, and green ingredients flaunting the colors of Mexico. And there was
uch more.

t one point I developed an earache. In my entire life I had never had an earache
re. Naturally my first inclination was to see an American-ish doctor. I saw one
was popular and was recommended by other expats. He prescribed some
ication, and I paid close to one hundred dollars (U.S.). A few days later, I still had
arache.

My amigas' noticed me wincing and rubbing at my ear. They took me to their
or. They warned me it would not be in the nicer tourist areas, but it was safe, and
as where locals went for simple stuff like an ear infection. Long story short, I saw
doctor, got medicine and was cured in a few days.

Time passes by.

Back at our apartment, my husband and I keep current with CNN news and ot
English-speaking television. Sometime in early 2020 we began hearing sto
about a virus that seemed to be spreading in different parts of the world. Every
days or so, the storyline and the spread seemed to grow and present m
significance.

Eventually we started hearing reports of cruise ships being quarantined,
need for people to dawn masks, implement social distancing, and that people
age and better were at risk, with potentially fatal outcomes. Certainly,
concerned us, but we were in a quandary of mixed messages.
For example, the news reported a specific cruise ship had been quarantined. W
looking through my binoculars off our balcony, I could see that same cruise s
docked in the harbor, full of tourists. Mask wearing and social distancing was no
affect anywhere we went. People were still doing peck like kisses on the cheek
the customary greeting. No businesses were shutting their doors or closing.

I asked my amigas about their community and what they felt about
virus/pandemic being reported. They were not too concerned. For the most p
they believed if this was natural, then they would survive it. They had the s
tequila, and other healthy habits.
Meanwhile, my husband and I, especially me, began to panic. We were not in
U.S., and although we were both healthy and strong, we did not want to contr
this virus and end up in a Mexican hospital where we knew nothing, were not flu
in the language, and only knew a few people.

New virus updates were reported daily on every English-speaking station
panic was building in many parts of the world. People were dying and it was bad.
Yet, in Mexico, at least where we were, still there was no signs of panic or conce
That is until one day in late March 2020, the leader of the country announ
everything was to close, immediately.

My husband and I had already been discussing whether we should leave. WI
the official announcement for businesses to close was made, we immediat
scheduled flights back to the U.S.

A day or so later, we were notified that our flights had been cancelled, and according to the locals that we knew, there were rumors that borders were also closing, which meant we could not drive or fly.

My husband and I had complete panic at the idea that we may be stuck in Mexico, and unable to return to the U.S., amidst a deadly pandemic that we were at risk for.

And so, with our local connections, we were able to get a driver for hire. We drove back to the U.S. two days later.

Our harrowing drive returning to the U.S. is a whole other story that I may post at another time.

Now that we have resettled in the U.S. and survived the pandemic, I was ready for another, new thang. Shaving my hair has been very liberating.

This 40-page story is a metaphorical gem.

It is a journey for your senses, and it is worth taking!

This is my gift to anyone who has ever experienced losing a loved one.

The South Side Of Heaven

By Stella St

Stella Stella

Many required readings in college included commonly known American Literarie Hemingway, Poe, Steinbeck, Wells, etc.). All were great writers and I have no kno against them. However, their stories were too abstract for my life. Within the rea Literature, there is room for those/us who have a different background, a differe perspective, and a passion for reading and writing".

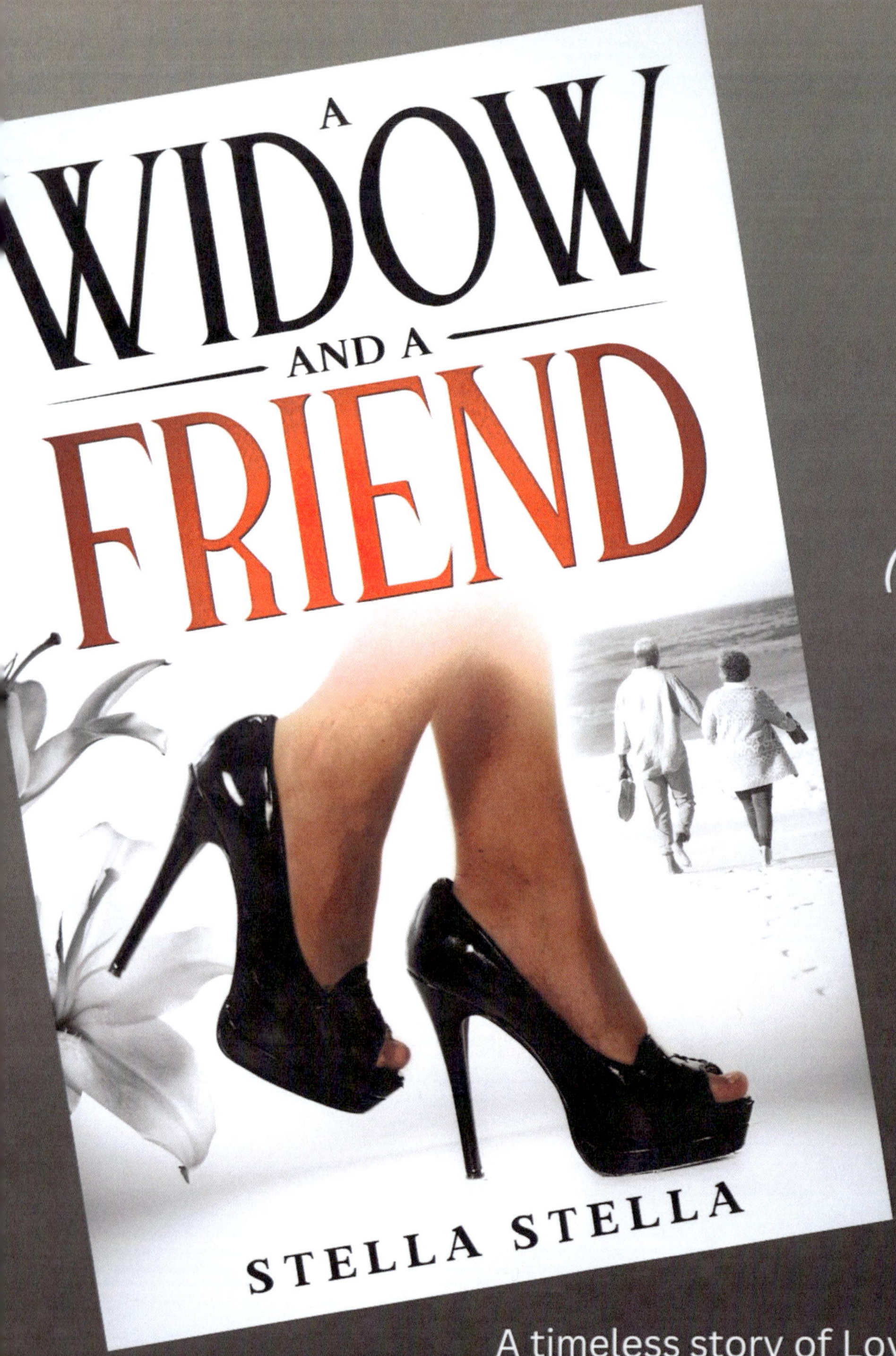

A WIDOW AND A FRIEND

STELLA STELLA

Love,

Romance,

& Friendship

(with a Twist)

Prepare to have your own paradigms challenged.

A timeless story of Love, Romance, and Friendship. Follow the journey of sixty-one-year-old, Tina Mason, as she navigates the loss of her husband. On the same day of his funeral, a knock at the door presents her with a quandary – a different opportunity to grieve.

PS – If this was a screenplay, I know who I would cast. Who would you cast?

BWA's Top Emerging Authors

AUTHOR

CONITRA COWANS

Bio

eautiful people, my name is Conitra
ns and I'm so excited to be apart of
I'm embarking on my journey as
ime author, my book I Didn't Know
s my Worth will be launched on July
had an opportunity to have my
r mentor Lacole Smith help me pour
y emotions on paper. I didn't Know
nonfiction book to help or give
rces to someone who has been
gh obstacles and challenges in life.
your self worth and let no one take
rom you. Just know that you are
h.

About My Book

This book shares with you my journey, and
why I was questioning my worth, but now I
finally realize MY WORTH! If you are
questioning your worth, I hope this book helps
you find your worth as well. I wanted to share
my journey with you from my early years to
how I got to where I am today. I can honestly
say that the journey wasn't easy, but now I
know it was necessary.

Bio:

Latasha About the author: Latasha is minister, an educator, a professionalism and life coach, a business owner, a inspirational speaker but most of all, child of the Most High God. Her desire to help as many people as possible on th journey we call life.

These journals were created with people like me in mind You know what you need but you ar not always sure where to find i Those of us on a journey to g deeper in our walk with God but jus need a little help. It is my sincer desire that this journal helps you o your path and becomes another too in your toolbox of life. I pray thes scriptures, reflections, confirmation and affirmations become a part o you every day life. Be bless!

Author
Chilita Perkins

Chilita Perkins was born and raised in Chicago, Illinois, to Eugene and Vicki Cunningham. [A]t a young age, she was trained for ministerial duties under Elder Titus and the late [___]ia Anderson at The Holy Covenant Church of God in Christ. Despite growing up in a [home] affected by domestic violence, Chilita's mother, an Evangelist at Liberty Tabernacle All [Natio]ns Church (LTANC), instilled in her the values and strength needed to stand as a child of [God.] Following her family's separation from LTANC, Chilita faced numerous challenges and [made] several life-altering decisions that led her astray. She endured her own battles with [dome]stic violence and family abuse but found solace and focus through activities such as [___] drill teams and dance groups. On November 24, 1994, Chilita recommitted herself to [Chris]t New Birth Outreach Ministry under Pastor Rayford Pointer. By the age of 22, she was [ordain]ed as a minister of the gospel. During her time at New Birth Outreach Ministry, Chilita [earned] a certificate of Training for Service and became a head teacher and organizer for the [child]ren's Ministry and VBS summer programs. Mentored by the head intercessor, Dr. Mildred [___]s, Chilita developed into a prayer warrior and a strong, resilient woman. Together with [her e]x-husband, she engaged in street evangelism and taught evangelism classes to other [minis]tries.

Chilita has been recognized for her community activism with medals and certificates from Ar Duncan of the Chicago Public Schools (CPS) and has served as a community activist for eight ye under Developing Community Projects (DCP). She co-founded the Second Chance Organization the homeless and neglected souls, and established The Vision Dance Production for you Additionally, she is a licensed educator, barber, and stylist. As an entrepreneur, she owned seve shops titled "Chi Town's Finest Beauty and Barber Shop" in Illinois and Arizona, Currently, works as a government official. In 2005, Chilita founded Rhema Word Christian Center, where attended classes on the Apostolic Faith and The School of the Prophets. In 2006, she was called God as a Prophetess and was later ordained by Apostle Isaac Perkins of Rhema Word Christ Center and Apostle Lopez of Mahanaim New Birth. Prophetess Chilita Perkins is known for anointing in prophetic worship, deliverance, breakthrough, and restoration under the guidance the Holy Spirit. She taught and preached the RHEMA WORD of God through prophetic teachir Through life's challenges, she discovered her true calling as a writer, authoring several boc including "Don't Be Afraid to Tell," "The Black Sheep Has Two Faces," "Black America," "Life Af Adultery," and her work-in-progress, "Becoming a Woman." Additionally, she is a motivatio speaker and social media influencer, hosting a live podcast titled "The Unlocked Chest," featured Facebook, YouTube, and Instagram. No longer preaching in traditional church settings, Chi Perkins continues to lead by example, meeting people where they are with truth and respect. was married to Apostle Isaac Perkins for over 26 years. A loving mother to three children, one her sons a marine and grandmother to five grandsons

WHAT'S COOKING?

Three delicious recipes to add to your menu

Spicy Chicken Tacos

Ingredients:

1 lb chicken breasts, boneless and skinless

1 tbsp olive oil

1 tbsp chili powder

1 tsp cumin

1 tsp paprika

1/2 tsp garlic powder

1/2 tsp onion powder

1/2 tsp salt

1/4 tsp black pepper

8 small tortillas

1 cup shredded lettuce

1/2 cup diced tomatoes

1/4 cup chopped red onions

1/2 cup shredded cheese

1/4 cup sour cream

1 lime, cut into wedges

Fresh cilantro, chopped (optional)

Cooking Instructions:

Prepare the Chicken: Cut the chicken breasts into small, bite-sized pieces.

Season the Chicken: In a bowl, combine chili powder, cumin, paprika, garlic powder, onion powder, salt, and black pepper. Mix well and coat the chicken pieces with the spice mixture.

Cook the Chicken: Heat olive oil in a large skillet over medium-high heat. Add the seasoned chicken and cook for about 7-10 minutes, or until the chicken is fully cooked and slightly crispy on the edges.

Warm the Tortillas: In another skillet, warm the tortillas over low heat until they are soft and pliable.

Assemble the Tacos: Place a generous amount of chicken in each tortilla. Top with shredded lettuce, diced tomatoes, chopped red onions, shredded cheese, and a dollop of sour cream.

Serve: Garnish with lime wedges and fresh cilantro, if desired. Serve immediately and enjoy your spicy chicken tacos!

CLASSIC BEEF STEW

Classic Beef Stew

Ingredients:

- 2 lbs beef chuck, cut into 1-inch cubes
- 3 tbsp flour
- 2 tbsp olive oil
- 1 large onion, chopped
- 2 cloves garlic, minced
- 4 cups beef broth
- 1 cup red wine (optional)
- 3 large carrots, peeled and cut into chunks
- 4 medium potatoes, peeled and cut into chunks
- 2 celery stalks, chopped
- 1 cup frozen peas
- 2 tbsp tomato paste
- 1 tbsp Worcestershire sauce
- 1 tsp dried thyme
- 1 bay leaf
- Salt and pepper to taste
- Fresh parsley, chopped (optional)

Cooking Instructions:

1. Prepare the Beef: Toss the beef cubes in flour, coating them evenly.
2. Brown the Beef: In a large pot, heat olive oil over medium-high heat. Add the beef cubes and brown them on all sides. Remove the beef from the pot set aside.
3. Sauté the Vegetables: In the same pot, add the chopped onion and minced garlic. Sauté until the onion is translucent.
4. Add Liquids: Pour in the beef broth and red wine scraping the bottom of the pot to release any browned bits.
5. Combine Ingredients: Return the browned beef the pot. Add carrots, potatoes, celery, tomato paste Worcestershire sauce, thyme, bay leaf, salt, and pepper. Stir well.
6. Simmer: Bring the stew to a boil, then reduce the heat to low. Cover and simmer for 2 hours, stirring occasionally, until the beef is tender and the vegetables are cooked through.
7. Add Peas: In the last 10 minutes of cooking, add frozen peas.
8. Serve: Remove the bay leaf. Serve the stew hot, garnished with fresh parsley if desired. Enjoy your hearty classic beef stew!

ECIPE #3 CREAMY
USHROOM RISOTTO

ny Mushroom Risotto

dients:

1/2 cups Arborio rice

cups chicken or vegetable broth

cup white wine

tbsp olive oil

small onion, finely chopped

cloves garlic, minced

cups mushrooms, sliced

2 cup grated Parmesan cheese

4 cup heavy cream

tbsp butter

alt and pepper to taste

resh parsley, chopped (optional)

ooking Instructions:

eat the Broth: In a saucepan, heat the

hicken or vegetable broth and keep it

arm over low heat.

auté the Vegetables: In a large skillet or

ot, heat olive oil over medium heat. Add

he chopped onion and minced garlic,

nd sauté until the onion is translucent.

ook the Mushrooms: Add the sliced

ushrooms to the skillet and cook until

hey are soft and golden brown

Toast the Rice: Add the Arborio rice to the skillet, stirring constantly until the rice is lightly toasted.

1. Deglaze with Wine: Pour in the white wine, stirring until it is mostly absorbed by the rice.

2. Add Broth Gradually: Add a ladleful of warm broth to the rice, stirring continuously until the liquid is mostly absorbed. Repeat this process, adding broth one ladleful at a time, until the rice is creamy and cooked through (about 18-20 minutes).

3. Finish with Cream and Cheese: Stir in the grated Parmesan cheese, heavy cream, and butter. Season with salt and pepper to taste.

4. Serve: Serve the risotto hot, garnished with fresh parsley if desired. Enjoy your creamy mushroom risotto!

Author
Lawanda Banks

Bio

Lawanda Banks is a multifaceted professional known for her roles as an a certified te
in the State of Texas, entrepreneur, and published author. With a career spanning ove
decades in education, Lawanda began her journey in 2000 and holds a Seco
Education Teaching Certification from Mico Teachers College in Kingston, Jamaica
furthered her academic pursuits with a Bachelor of Science Degree in University St
from the University of Texas at Arlington.

In addition to her work in education, Lawanda is the proud owner and lead instructor o
Start Kindergarten Prep LLC, also known as First Start Tutoring LLC. Her dedicati
nurturing young minds extends beyond the classroom, reflecting her passio
educational empowerment and student success.

Beyond her professional endeavors, Lawanda is recognized for her artistic flair, crec
and talent, which she infuses into her teaching and entrepreneurial ventures. Ground
faith, spirituality, and a commitment to self-empowerment, Lawanda Banks continu
inspire and impact her community through her innovative educational approache

Author, Motivational & Empowerment Speaker
Tonya GRAVES-Beasley

...een writing books for many years and recently started publishing, this year, 2024. My ...ublished book for Reading Is titled "Your Drug of Choice, the elephant in the room". Next ...is "You are more than a Paper Pusher" – this one is for behind the scene workers ...cially those ...ng in ministry; and then we have "More Than a Paper Pusher" - this one is for ...rs/pastors, ...which are available on Amazon. There will be three more released later this year ...ling a ...en series all listed under Pen Name "Beasley Bee"

...the Founder of two Non-Profit Organizations "Youth Preparing 4 Success" and then ...sing on Hope, Inc" I am the Birth Mother of Three, known as My Gifts and they are My ...ration. My pass time is spent with my mom and my grandbabies and then there are my ...d babies. I love to serve, and I Love to sing. My free time is spent Reading, Writing, ...oring and posting encouragement ...s on my YouTube Channel "Enjoying Talks with L & B". However lately I've been called ...to ...e do group sessions and speaking at events to get the conversation started as it relates to ...st ..."Your Drug of Choice, the elephant in the room". For more information please visit my ...ite ...Beasleybee.com and then my organization website: ...youthpreparing4successinc.org

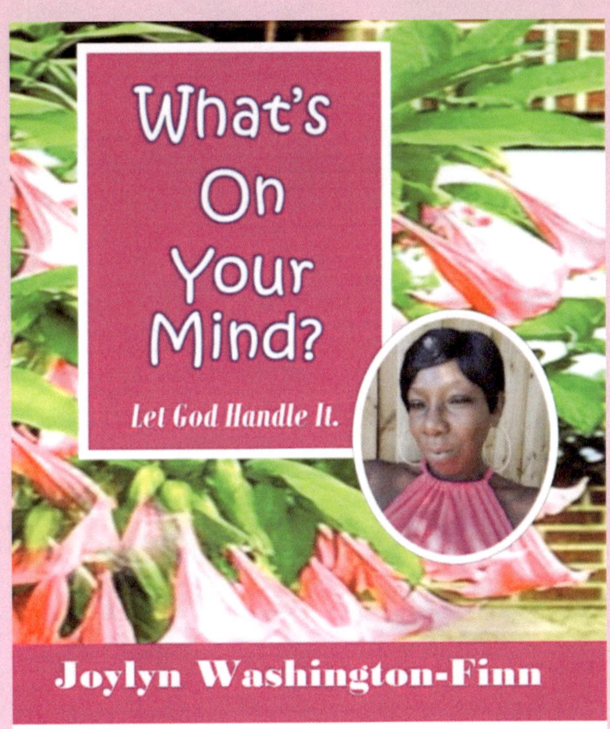

Book overview

What's On Your Mind? Let God Handle It.
Thinking, talking, crying, expressing what's on your mind.
Joylyn Washington-Finn offers you a little carry-along
to keep track of how you' take it to your
Father in Heaven' – Who loves you and hears you toda
any day, anywhere, anytime.
Looking for answers? **Let God Handle It!**

About the author

Follow authors to get new release updates, plus
improved recommendations.

Joylyn Washington-Finn

Following

God's daughter, a Mother, Grandma, Sister, Friend,
Author. Challenges have been overcome. Still fighting
for the Lord. Determined to keep praising His name, o
Father God. From the Ohio hills to the Florida water, a
his creations, as our we. I love you! Joylyn Washington
Finn.

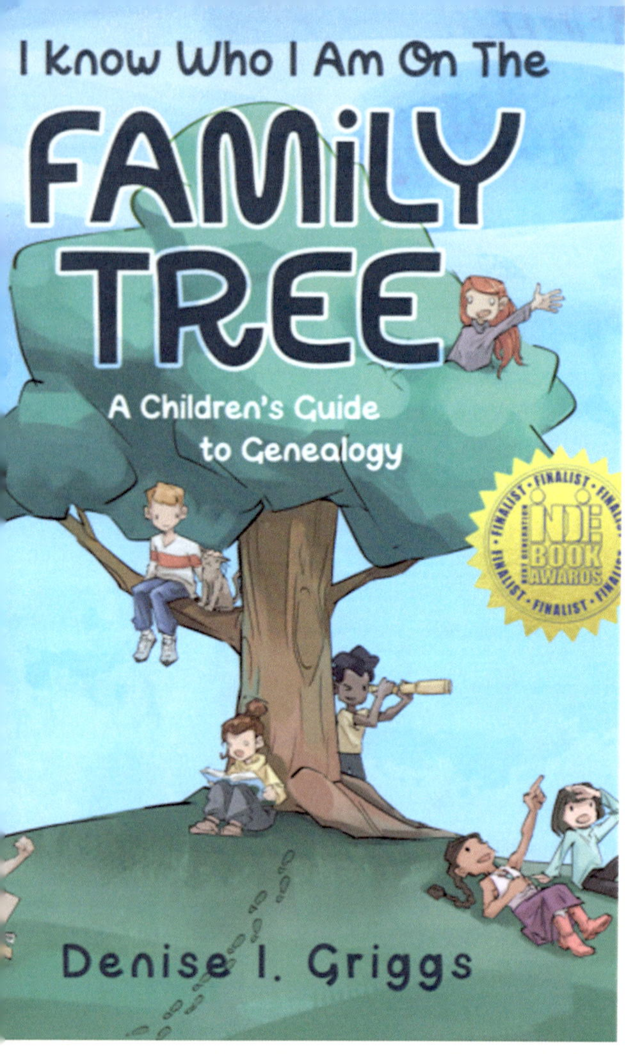

s book will help children and
ents work together to uncover
s about their ancestors and
y they fit into history,
graphy, and society. There are
s in everyone's family history
need to be solved. Some
stions might be: Why did
ilies stay where they lived, or
did they suddenly leave?
ere did they go? Were they
n a large continent or an exotic
nd? Where does your family
e originate? Why do you love
ain foods? Where did these
ds originate?
g this book will help locate
clues to answer the history
mysteries of your family. It
help families prepare for the
, or next family reunion!

Author
Denise Griggs

Denise Griggs is a family genealogist with 35 years of research, spanning ancestral roots in diverse countries like Africa, Europe, Australia, Ireland, and North America. Her maternal lineage traces back to eighth-century England and extends to southwest Mississippi.

She discovered the need to teach children the basics of genealogy through her book, I Know Who I Am On the Family Tree, A Children's Guide to Genealogy, for which she earned a Finalist Award in the Indie Book Awards. This work earned her the Next Generation Indie Book Award. Denise is also an author of children's books focusing on diversity and theology.

An advocate for history and heritage, Denise is actively involved in organizations like the Daughters of the American Revolution (DAR), volunteers with the National Park Service, and the Natchez U.S. Colored Troops Monument Committee in Mississippi. She serves as the Exhibit Chair on the board of the Greater Sacramento African American Genealogy Society, preserving and sharing cultural histories. Denise holds honors, with a B.A. and M.A. from a Christian University. She is the owner of Glass Tree Books® and Blue Eclipse Publishing®. Her genealogy presentations are also on her YouTube channel, D.I. Griggs Media.

Introduction:

VISIONARY * MENTOR *COACH * MOTIVATIONAL SPEAKER * DOMESTIC VIOLENCE ADVOCATE *BEST SELLING AUTHOR * MIDWIFE *NATIONAL SPOKESPERSON

Shacre Jones is not your average individual. She's a force to be reckoned with - an accomplished author, a captivating motivational speaker, and an unwavering advocate for raising awareness about domestic violence.

Residing in the Dover, Delaware region. Shacre Jones is a survivor of domestic abuse and thriving advocate passionate about women evolving after abuse. Through her ministry and writing, she fearlessly uses her voice to encourage, uplift, challenge, and

inspire people of all ages. With Jones's remarkable ability to connect with her audience on a deeply emotional level, she transforms into a powerful speaker who brings unparalleled depth and perspective to topics such as faith, family, relationships, domestic violence prevention, and personal development.

Author
Nikita Ford

My name is Nikita Ford, I was born and raised in Beloit, WI. I am a mother of 5 and grandmother of 5.

Rubies with a Purpose is my first book and I'm so excited so share my testimony and encourage other women. Being a survivor of domestic violence I wanted to write a book that reminds women that we are precious jewels and we all have a purpose in life no matter what we have been through.

Nikita Ford
Founder of Rubies with a Purpose
(502) 516-6937
rubieswithapurpose@gmail.com

Valerie Staton

Valerie D. Staton is an author/poet from New Jersey. She has writen two insightful books and contributed poetry and short stories to several books, anthologies, and online communities.

Her latest publication entitled "Staton the Facts - The Informative Bible-Based Activity Book" has over 1,200 activities. Readers will find within its pages word scrambles, word matches, word searches, speaker identification, bible verse completion and scripture based cryptogram puzzles to solve. Also included throughout this spectacular book are over one hundred fun biblical facts. Answer sheets in the back of the book contain reference text.

The author's first publication, "Odes of Praise - A Collection of Christian Poetry, consists of 86 awe-inspiring poems, edifying our Lord and Savior Jesus Christ.

These wonderful publications are available for purchase on Amazon.com.

Author
TONYA BAILEY

y name is Tonya Bagwell-Bailey and I am the Author of Pray Without Ceasing. It is a ayer journal that I wrote my own personal prayers with scriptures to follow. I share ys of how to pray, what to pray about and when to pray. At times we find ourselves situations where we don't know how to get out of them. Or even life causes you to ake decisions unknowingly. But I know a God who is our source will supply all our eds. God is our refuge and strength; he will not leave you or forsake you. The reason egan writing this journal was because I was going through something in my life that ok me to a dark place of stress and depression. I was diagnosed with breast cancer ile waiting for a kidney transplant. Yes, I questioned God and said, "Why me and y now?" God began to speak to me and said, because I know you are strong, and I l not put no more on you than you can bear so my child stand still and keep silent d let me do what I need to do. Every day I began to pray and write down what I ayed for followed with scripture. No, I didn't receive my kidney transplant, but I am ncer free. I am currently about to start Peritoneal Dialysis because I must wait five ars before I can receive a kidney, but God knows what you need when you need it. e response I receive from others on how my prayer journal has helped others has ally touched my heart.

ontact information:

nya Bagwell-Bailey

nya.bailey89@yahoo.com

SPOTLIGHT TUCKER

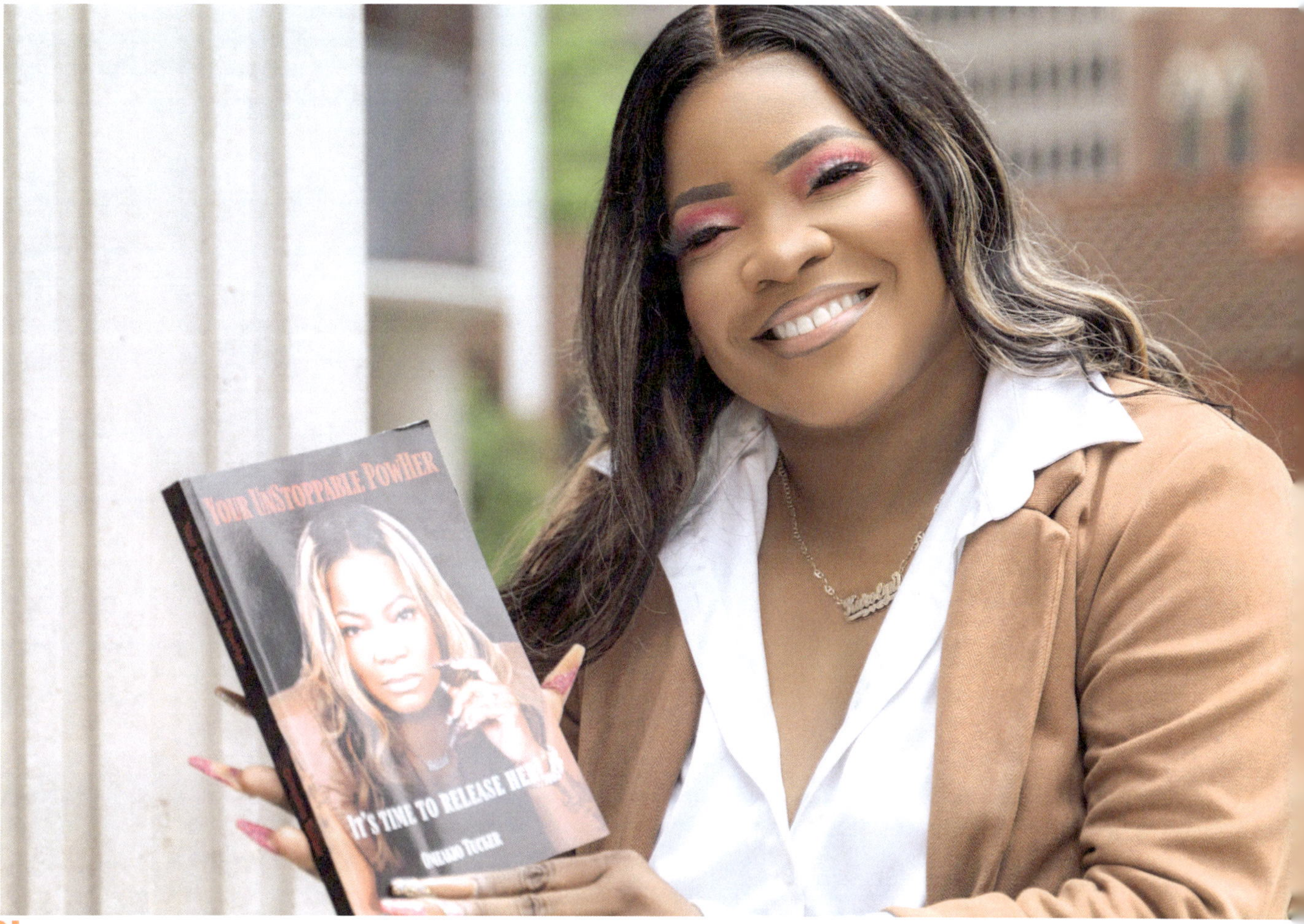

Bio

Omeakio Tucker, a new and upcoming author, fearlessly shares her personal journey of facing challenges, feeling stuck, and ultimately breaking free in her transformative book. Drawing from her own experiences and her deep connection with God, Omeakio is your cheerleader and guide, showing you that transformation is possible. This book is more than just another self-help guide; it's a heart-to-heart conversation and a loving reminder that you are capable of so much more than you ever thought possible. Omeakio will help you identify the limiting beliefs and patterns that have been holding you back and provide you with the tools you need to unleash your Unstoppable PowHer.

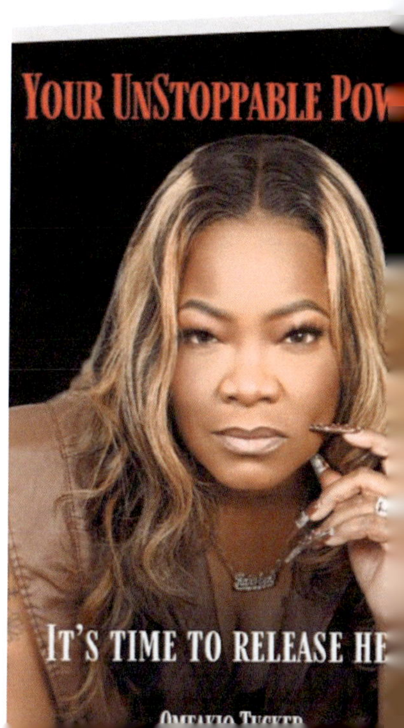

a Bachelor's Degree in Business
ninistration, a Master's Degree in
anizational Leadership, and certification
an Executive Coach and Consultant,
eakio brings a wealth of knowledge and
ertise to her writing. Her 20+ years of
erience as a dynamic manager, creative
ctor, passionate mentor, and influential
cutive in Corporate America have
ed her into a captivating mixture of
nts, making her an unstoppable force
the ultimate catalyst for meaningful
nge.

ed by her unwavering faith and
ionship with God, Omeakio pours life
inspiration into the community she
es with steadfast dedication. She
es in Dallas, TX, with her loving husband,
beautiful children, nine precious
dchildren, and the world's cutest
dpup. Her family is her rock and
ration, providing her with the
avering support and love that fuels her
sion to empower women worldwide.

Available on Amazon or for an autographed
copy purchase through my website

Allyna Robinson Hughley

Award-Winning, Self-Published Author

Is family oriented and the 11th of 13 children. She has been married for 31 years and has 2 sons. She has a Bachelor of Science degree in Computer Science. Allyna served in the United States Army Reserve for 20 years and is now retired. She is currently employed with the Department of Defense as an IT Applications Manager where supervises a team which designs and maintains IT systems and supports military personnel and their families worldwide. Allyna believes in empowering and uplifting the young community. She hopes her creative writing will inspire children to laugh, dream, and be the best version of themselves.

Soft Cover, Grades: Pre-K thru 5th, Juvenile Fiction, Children's Social and Emotional Book, Family Book

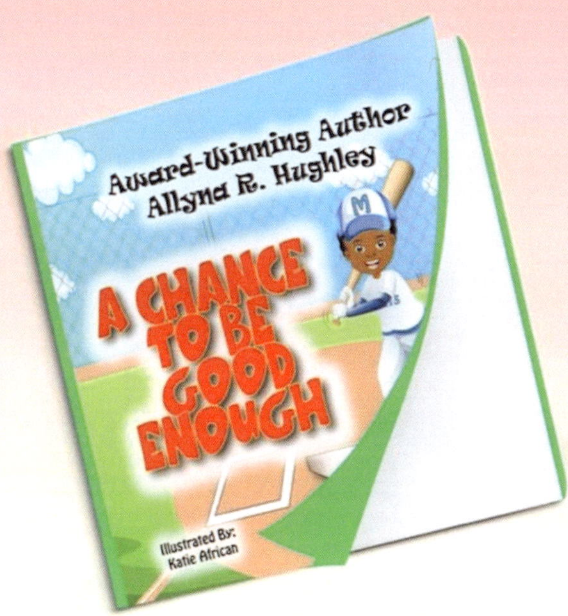

Children's books teach readers a valuable lesson about appreciation. They provide social and emotional learning for our children. The books help readers to understand and manage emotions, make responsible decisions, maintain positive relationships, and show empathy towards others.

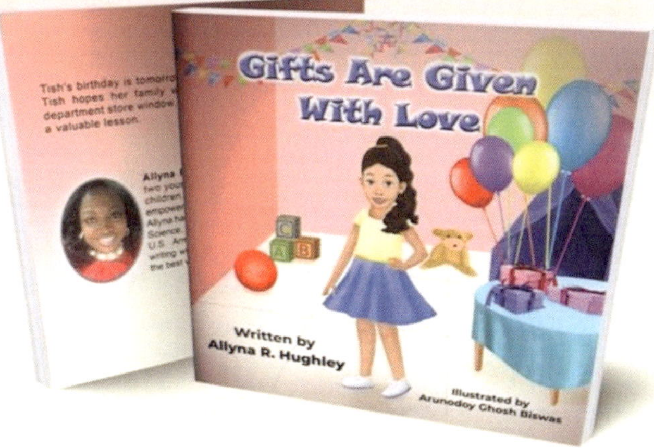

Contact: 757.717.3883
Website: Giftsaregivenwithlove.com
Instagram: @authorallynarhughley
Facebook: Author : Allyna R. Hughley

EKECIA
ORDHAM

kecia is a native of Charleston, S.C., d the founder of Lekecia Fordham nistries LLC, which is an extension her call to a life of worship and ows her to minister to God's people an author, public speaker, minister the gospel, blogger, and more. She a Christian Author that has recently blished her first book "Beautiful Lies The Ugly Truth: Escaping Bondage d Embracing Freedom in Truth", ich is currently available on nazon, IngramSpark, and her bsite: ww.lekeciafordhamministries.com. is book was designed to be a tool at unveils the lies of the enemy that sires to keep us ensnared in the kes of bondage. She undeniably derstands the power of words and at faith comes by hearing and by aring the word of God. In this vein, e is also the co-host of "Phone ggets Podcast" which is a cebook and YouTube platform that courages and edifies others in the ndrous Word of God.

BWA | Author
Lekecia Fordham

She is married to her love Richard and between them they have six wonderful children and five adorable grandchildren. Lekecia has always had a heart for others. As a child she desired to be a psychologist in hopes to help those hurting and suffering to cope with life. After giving her life to the Lord, that same desire and passion was revealed in the call to ministry. As a minister of the gospel, she ministers and comforts many in the faith by the grace of God. She finds her strength in the word of God and a life of prayer. She encourages others to know that with God all things are possible and that we can have a whole, complete, and full life in Him. Despite where you have been, if you allow Him, by faith God can make all things new. Her motto is … "Your failures were never intended to be a muzzle, but a bullhorn!".

Social Media

Instagram: Thelekeciafordham

Facebook: Lekecia Fordham

X (formerly Twitter): Lekeciafordham1

Amazon Book Link: https://amzn.to/4651PCv

Beautiful Lies Vs
The Ugly Truth:
Escaping Bondage And Embracing
Freedom In Truth
Minister Lekecia L. Fordham

Author Maria Grier

Pastor, Preacher,Life Coach,Mentor, Motivational, Prayer Warrior, Demon Slayer, Advocate For All Pec
Whom Deal Or Dealt with Trauma

Maria Grier is a trailblazer who defeats all odds. Maria is not your average woman. Def
is not an option for her. Maria walks very heavy in her call, as a strong dynamic leade
Pastor, Prophetess and Prayer Warrior. Maria has always had a strong thrive, hunger,
drive to motivate those she encounters to become an agent of change. She is sought a
by many for her dynamic preaching and teaching through her powerful speaking abili
to help others evolve from defeat to un-defeat from victim to victor through variou
events and resources through mentoring programs that help Empower Impact and ca
transformation in the life of the people she mentor.
Maria is the catalyst to see those defeat all odds stacked against them, Maria is a li
coach and mentors for those that survived childhood abuse and various traumas. H
childhood trauma causes her to walk bodly and fiercely being a warden that unlocks.

Maria Grier, Cont'd

a Grier (Harris) also known as Pastor/ Prophetess Grier is one of the leaders of
ne Room Global Ministries. She is honored to work in ministry alongside her
band of 26yrs, Bishop Kahlil Grier. In addition, Pastor Maria Grier is the mother of 3
utiful daughter's and have several God children and one granddaughter. Maria is a
ve of Dover, Delaware. Currently lives in the region of Texas.
essionally Maria has worked as a cosmetologist, receptionist, administrative
stant clerk and as a bus aide. Entrepreneurship has always been the ultimate goal for
a. In 2019 Bling- A- Bling Jewelry for All was launched, as a Independent Paparazzi
sultant for Paparazzi. Expanding Her entrepreneurship, she then open Tripl5 K
tique and printing. Now her dream. became her reality and has become a great
ion, of helping others start, their small businesses. Maria is a certified life coach,
vational speaker, preacher and teacher. Maria is a published Contributing Author of
ral books, such as "Throne Room Global Ministries Note Book Prayer In Pearland" ,
w To Pray For A Successful Marriage Volume II" & "Healing Through Brokenness."
a have established two amazing non-profit organizations in her communities "Freely
 Outreach Resource Center;" This organization help those in the community with
, clothing, shelter and help assist with resources we may have for those that are
able, if none are available they are resourced out to outside agencies. Her passion
elp those that dealt with trauma of any sort, due to her traumatic childhood, cause
birthing of Women Healed Of Abuse better know as WHOA. Two of greatest
mplishments thus far being a CEO/ Founder. Women Healed Of Abuse help mentor
sist Women and Men, as well as children that have battled or battling abused,
er mentally abuse, emotionally abuse, verbally abuse and sexually abuse. She wants
rs to know through her organization that you are no longer a victim , but a Victor
you can heal and become a winner in life. Jeremiah 31:3 says "The Lord hath
eared of old unto me, saying yeah I have loved thee with an everlasting love;
efore with lovingkindness have I drawn thee, which motivates and gives Maria the
e to keep striving for God excellence daily. God has truly shown her Psalms 147:3 He
d) healed her broken heart and wounds. Pastor Maria is a bold, strong, fierce woman
 great worth and inspiration to all she encounters, as she always quote " What God
For Me(her), It is For Me (her). Which in December God saw fit for Maria to be
ded the Presidential Lifetime Achievement Award and addition she also recieved a
d from the City Of Houston for all her amazing community efforts around the
ounding areas of Houston.
a is very excited, to see what other things God will have her to do, that will Enhance
mpact, Empower the people she comes in contact with on her life.

Standard & Specialty Vinyl Designs

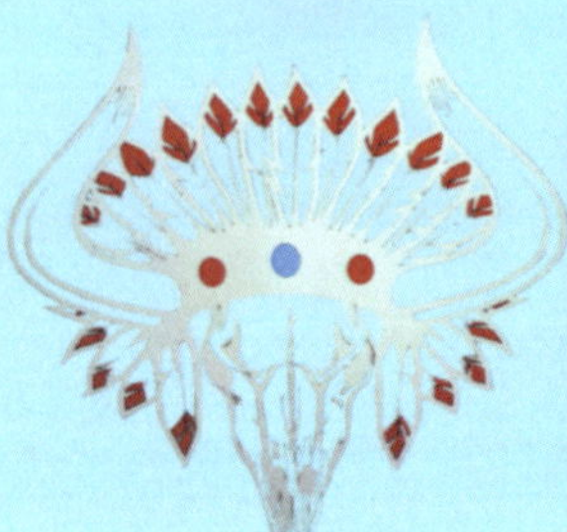

Sublimation & Direct to Film

Stickers & Decals

Paulette's Journals Available on Amazon.com

Unlock the power of self-discovery and personal growth with our thoughtfully crafted journal books designed to ignite your creativity and transform your life. Whether you're an aspiring writer or someone seeking to embark on a journey of self-exploration, our journal books are the perfect companions on your path to fulfillment. Within the pages of these beautifully designed journals, you'll find inspiring prompts, creative exercises, and guided reflections that will help you unlock your innermost thoughts and channel them into meaningful words. Embrace the cathartic process of putting pen to paper, unleash your imagination, and witness the incredible evolution of your writing and personal development. Your journey awaits—start creating the life you've always envisioned, one insightful journal entry at a time.

Created by Paulette Henson, Available on Amazon.com

BWA
BLACK WOMEN AUTHORS
AUTHOR SPOTLIGHT
Annie Abrams
Jerwanda Johnson
Omeakio Tucker
Thandisizwe Chimurenga
Valerie Staton
ARTICLES
HEALTHY LIVING &
STRESS MANAGEMENT
The Game of Life!
The Writer's Guide to Staying Healthy!
BWA'S EMERGING AUTHORS & MORE
FEATURED AUTHOR
VICTORIA PEARSON
THE AI REVOLUTION

BWA
MAGAZINE
BLACK WOMEN AUTHORS
ARTICLES
LIVING WITH LUPUS
AUTHOR'S LOUNGE INTERVIEW
FEATURED AUTHOR
AKIYA MASTON
AUTHOR SPOTLIGHT
VICTORIA PEARSON

FEATURED AUTHOR
NADIA DOZIER
BOOK DEBUT:
CALLED TO BE A WIFE
KINGS CORNER
CE HOLMES
OB HORTON
ARTICLES:
FROM BLANK PAGE TO
BEST SELLER
SAY IT LOUD WITH
LITERATURE &
MORE!
BWA
MAGAZINE
AUTHOR SPOTLIGHT
OB LYNCH
TINA JACKSON
TEEKA TOLIVER
SHAUNTAH JONES
BLACK WOMEN AUTHORS

BWA
MAGAZINE
BLACK WOMEN AUTHORS
MAY 2024
HAPPY MOTHER'S DAY!
POETESS
TINA L. JACKSON
AUTHOR SPOTLIGHT
TEEKA TOLLIVER
VALERIE STATON
CELEBRATING POETS AUTHORS & MOTHERS

BWA
MAGAZINE
CELEBRATES
BLACK HISTORY
REMEMBERING HISTORICAL AUTHORS
MAYA ANGELOU
TONI MORRISON
AUTHOR SPOTLIGHT
CHERISE BURRELL
TALONA COLEMAN
JAMILA SMITH
TANYA STROKES
DR. LORENA NEWSON
FEATURED AUTHOR | POET
CLARISE ANNETTE BROOKS
PHENOMENAL WOMEN

SPECIAL EDITION
BWA
THE AUTHOR'S LOUNGE
Highlights:
Stephanie Bailey
Author Spotlight
Dr. Lorena Newson
Writing Tips
Kings Corner
The Poet's Lounge | Podcast
SUMMER 2023

BWA
Holiday
EDITION
#1 BEST SELLING
Author
Stephanie Bailey
TOP 25 EMERGING AUTHORS
Debra Simpson
Rose Jackson-Beavers
CELEBRATE LITERATURE
DECEMBER 2023

BLACK MEN AUTHORS
BMA
MAGAZINE
A TRIBUTE TO:
THE HARLEM RENAISSANCE
LANGSTON HUGHES
JAMES BALDWIN
CLAUDE MCKAY
CELEBRATING BLACK ART BUSINESSES & BRANDS
CELEBRATING BLACK HISTORY
FEATURING
OMAR TYREE
THE RENISSANCE MAN
BLACK MEN AUTHORS MAGAZINE

BMA
BLACK MEN AUTHORS
MAGAZINE
BRUCE GEORGE
GENIUS IS COMMON!
CO-FOUNDER OF DEF POETRY JAM
PREMIER EDITION
EMPOWER & INSPIRE
LITERARY TIPS, TRAVEL & MORE
AUTHORS & POETS SPOTLIGHT

HOLIDAY 2023
VOL. 1
FASHION MAGAZINE
SLAY
LIVING YOUR BEST LIFE IN STYLE

Books by
PAULETTE HENSON

ALL AVAILABLE ON AMAZON.COM

Salon Management & Business Essentials

Laila Goes to Dance Class

Daddy Issues

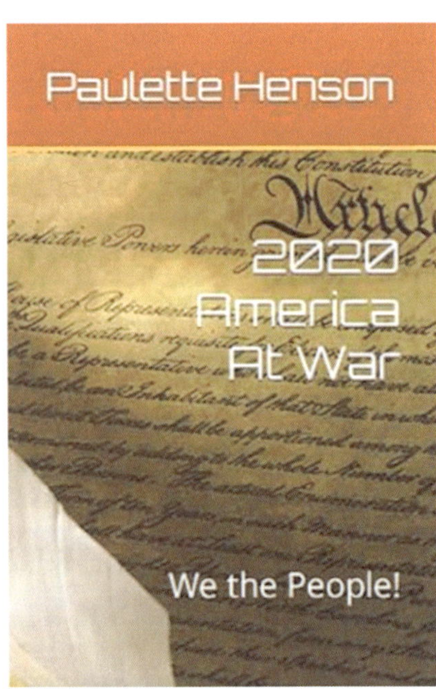

2020 America At War!

Smart Kids Activity Book

More Hair | Life of a Hairdresser

Support BWA

BWA LIBRARY

ALL AVAILABLE ON AMAZON.COM

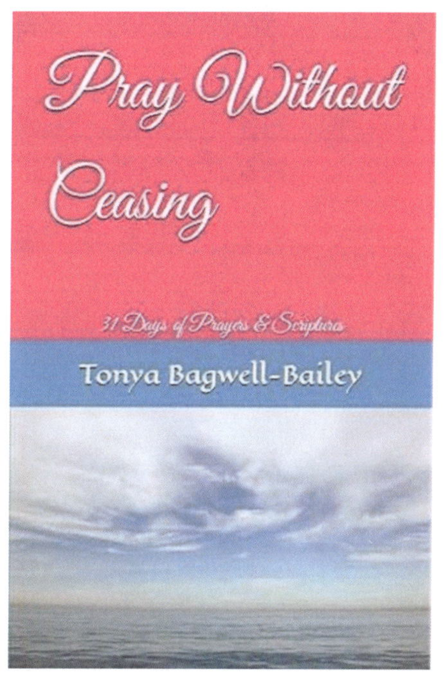

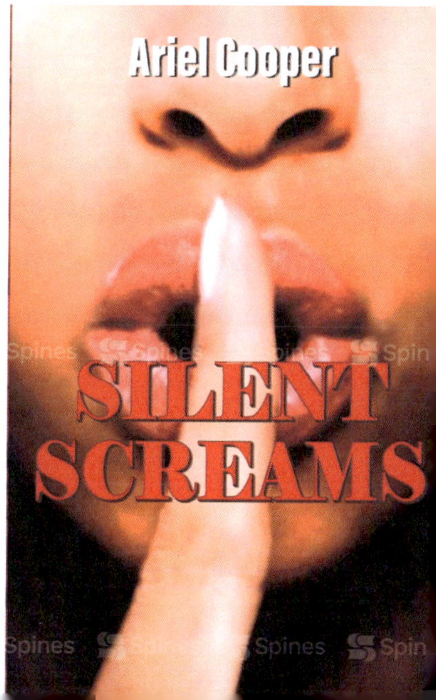

BWA LIBRARY

ALL AVAILABLE ON AMAZON.COM

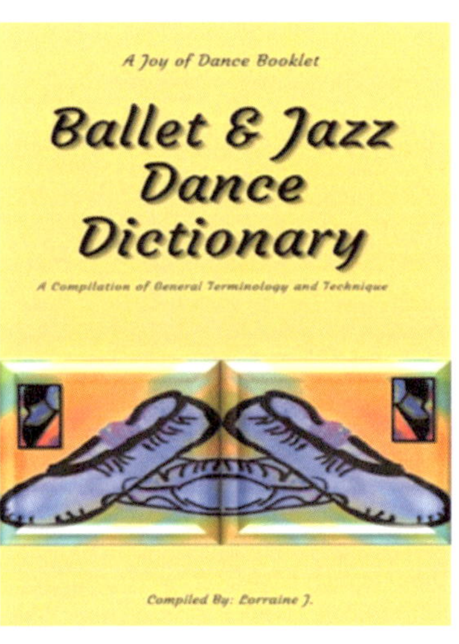

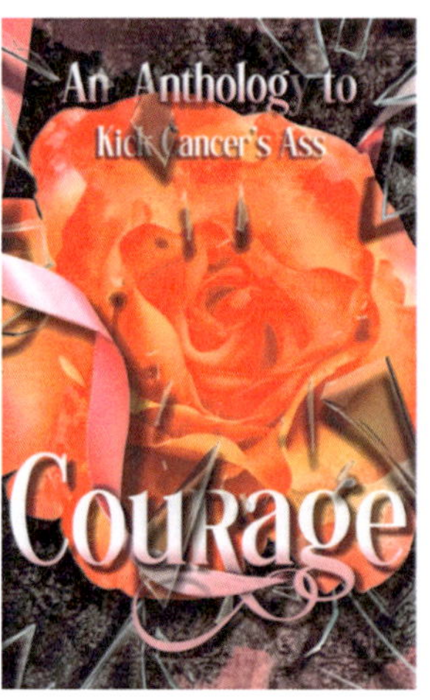

theauthorsloungetvshow@gmail.com

Victoria Anderson
More Than Your Trauma
A Personal Growth Journey for Young Black Women: Restoring Your Inner Child & Inner Peace

Trauma Recovery Workbook

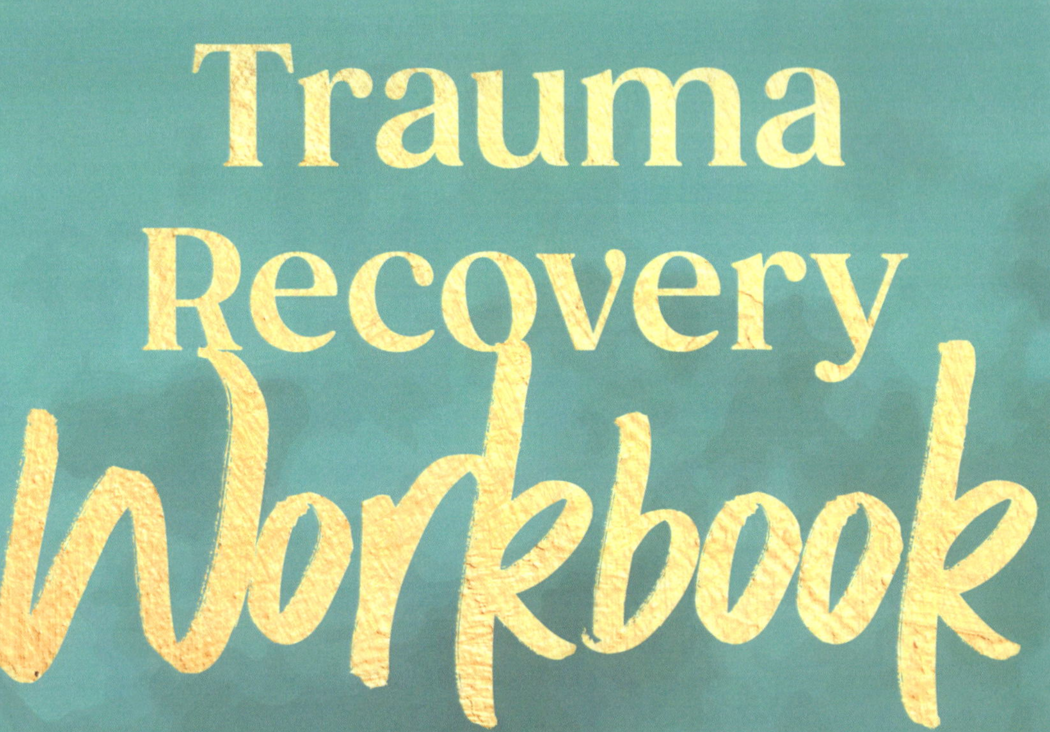

A Companion Journal to More Than Your Trauma.

Victoria Anderson

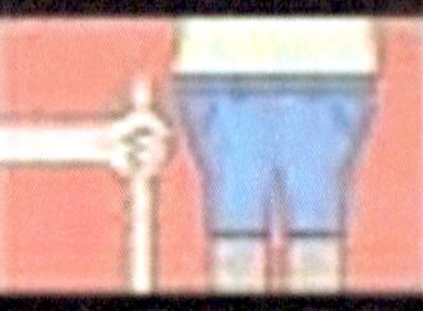

PRODUCTION

THE WONDER YEARS OF MIDDLE SCHOOL

SCENE
6TH – 8TH

DIRECTOR:
YOU

AUTHOR

AKIYA MASTON

POETRY IS LIFE!
NAIROBI
PAULETTE
HOST
TINA
CO-HOST
ACE HOLMES
2 AUG 2024
ROME
THE POET'S LOUNGE
OPEN MIC
OMAR TYREE
TEECH
2 AUG
CLARISE ANNETTE BROOKS
HOSTED BY
PAULETTE HENSON
CO-HOST TINA JACKSON
FACEBOOK/YOUTUBE LIVE
POETS/STUDIO GUEST ONLY
ZOOM MEETING ID#
843 6742 4989
FRIDAY 4PM (PST)
7PM EASTERN
5PM MOUNTAIN
6PM CENTRAL

POETRY IS LIFE!
NAIROBI
PAULETTE
HOST
TINA
CO-HOST
ACE HOLMES
6 SEP 2024
ROME
THE POET'S LOUNGE
OPEN MIC
OMAR TYREE
TEECH
2 AUG
CLARISE ANNETTE BROOKS
HOSTED BY
PAULETTE HENSON
CO-HOST TINA JACKSON
FACEBOOK/YOUTUBE LIVE
POETS/STUDIO GUEST ONLY
ZOOM MEETING ID#
843 6742 4989
FRIDAY 4PM (PST)
7PM EASTERN
5PM MOUNTAIN
6PM CENTRAL

Support Black Literature

FOLLOW US:
BLACK WOMEN AUTHORS/GROUP/FACEBOOK.COM

THE AUTHOR'S LOUNGE

PODCAST

WATCH:YOUTUBE/FACEBOOK "THE AUTHORS LOUNGE TV SHOW

The Poet's Lounge/Facebook.com

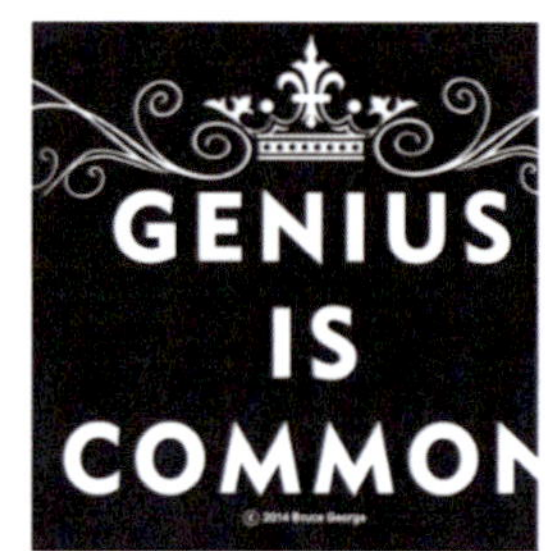

Blackwomenauthors.org

BWA - Black Women Authors

blackwomenauthors.org

Black Women Authors

Black Women Authors

Black Women Authors

Black Women Authors

Proud of my Island
Turks & Caicos Island

Black Women Authors

Black Women Authors

Black Women Authors

Giving Thanks to God for this Vision

With heartfelt gratitude, I lift my voice in thanks to God for his divine vision that has brought such extraordinary authors and poets to my midst. Their brilliance and creativity have enriched my life and the lives of countless others. I am humbled by the gift of their presence and the beauty they bring to the literary world.

I give thanks to God for orchestrating the perfect alignment of circumstances that allowed me to connect with these wonderful souls. It is a true testament to His divine plan and the power of His guiding hand. I am in awe of the ways in which God has brought us together, weaving a tapestry of talent, wisdom, and inspiration that continues to uplift and inspire us all.I

In this moment of gratitude, I acknowledge God's grace and providence for granting me the opportunity to collaborate and learn from these gifted authors and poets. Their unique voices and perspectives have illuminated my path and broadened my horizons. I am eternally grateful for the privilege of sharing this journey with them and witnessing the transformative impact of their words on the world. May we continue to be guided by God's wisdom and love as we journey together, united by our shared passion for literature, the writtenand spoken word.

DIVA

BLACK WOMEN AUTHORS
PAULETTE HENSON